Did you know...?

100 quirky facts about County Offaly

by Amanda Pedlow

GW00482776

Published by Offaly County Council
November 2013

Offaly County Council
Áras an Chontae
Charleville Road
Tullamore, Co. Offaly

Cover photo credits as applies

ISBN 978-0-9574533-3-3

Ordnance Survey maps,
license no. 2010/32/CCMA/OffalyCountyCouncil

Graphic Design by Connie Scanlon and James Fraher,
Bogfire, www.bogfire.com

This project was part funded by the Heritage Council under the
County Heritage Grant Scheme in 2013.

An Chomhairle Oidhreachta
The Heritage Council

Contents

Introduction

This book presents 100 quirky facts about Offaly. It gives a flavour of the wide spectrum of Offaly's heritage from geology to natural heritage and archaeology to architecture. The Heritage Office compiled this book with much material provided by Caimin O'Brien, archaeologist with the National Monuments Service, Dept of Arts, Heritage & the Gaeltacht: John Feehan, and Michael Byrne of the Offaly Historical and Archaeological Society. Stephen Heery provided text for the Shannon Callows, Stephen McNeill gathered information on railways, Aidan O'Sullivan of Dept of Archaeology UCD assisted with the Clonmacnoise Bridge entry and the National Biodiversity Centre supplied material about the Painted Lady Butterfly.

Illustrations were gathered far and wide with many thanks to all who assisted. Catherine Martin drew up the Making Offaly map. Mary Ann Williams did additional research and word-smithed much of the book. We are very grateful to Connie Scanlon and James Fraher from Bogfire for the design and a large number of the photographs used. Any unintentional errors or omissions are the responsibility of the Heritage Office.

Sincere thanks to all of the landowners who have facilitated survey work and visits made by the Heritage Office over the years. The welcome and information provided is always very much appreciated. Sites that are mentioned in the book that can be visited are listed on page 206. Please always check with landowners before visiting any sites on private land.

Did you know? 100 quirky facts about County Offaly is the most recent publication by Offaly County Council to promote our county's heritage and it draws on much material published over the past decade, including: *Living Under Thatch* (2004) by Barry O'Reilly; *Stories from a Sacred Landscape* (2006) by Caimin O'Brien; *The Wildflowers of Offaly* (2009), *Croghan* (2011) and *The Geology of Laois and Offaly* (2013) by John Feehan; and *Geashill, The Evolution of Its Architecture* (2012) by Rachel McKenna.

In recent years, online resources, such as www.archaeology.ie, www.buildingsofireland.ie, www.npws.ie and www.osi.ie, have transformed access to information about our county. Surveys by Fred Hamond of all the mills and bridges in County Offaly are available online at www.offaly.ie/heritage, as well as in the County Library. If you would like further information or sources for information published do contact the Heritage Office.

Our thanks to the South Dublin Association of An Taisce and Dún Laoghaire-Rathdown County Council, which produced the first *Did you know?* in 2009 and gave us permission to produce an Offaly version. We would like to thank the Heritage Council for its ongoing support of the promotion of Offaly heritage.

Amanda Pedlow
Offaly Heritage Officer
Offaly County Council
Áras an Chontae
Charleville Road
Tullamore, Co. Offaly
November 2013

Did you know . . .

After his travels abroad, Lieutenant Colonel Richard Wellesley Bernard of Kinnitty Castle decided that only one design would do for his family's mausoleum: that of the Pyramid of Cheops. Constructed between 1830-1834 to the rear of St Finan's Graveyard, the pyramid-shaped Kinnitty Mausoleum serves as the final resting place of six members of the Bernard family. The last was interred in 1907.

Offaly's second pyramid can be found at Sculpture in the Parklands, part of Lough Boora Parklands. During the 2002 International Sculpture Symposium, artist Eileen MacDonagh, assisted by Marc Wouters, created the stepped pyramid, which is 8 m wide and stands 6 m high. The pyramid is built from stones left behind when glaciers moved across Offaly. Buried for thousands of years by growing bogs, the glacial stone was revealed during peat harvesting.

Left: *Boora Pyramid* by Eileen MacDonagh (James Fraher)
Right: Kinnitty Mausoleum (James Fraher)

. . . that Offaly has two pyramids?

The Geashill Anemone

A garden favourite, the St Brigid anemone features double petals in scarlet, violet, blue and white. During the late 1800s, William Reamsbottom, of Alderborough Nursery in Geashill, developed 30 different colours of this flower and increased the number of double-petalled varieties.

Reamsbottom was married to Mary Enraght Mooney of The Doon, Ballinahown. Tradition says that he worked with anemone stock from her family's walled garden. His St Brigid anemone varieties won an award of merit at the Royal Horticultural Society of London (1902) and a gold medal at the Shrewsbury Show (1903).

During the early 1900s, the Alderborough Nursery was a substantial enterprise, employing up to 106 workers. As well as propagating plants, the workers had their own football team and dramatic society.

Left: Anemone Coronaria, Linnaeus 'Saint Brigid' which was grown in Geashill by William Reamsbottom of Alderborough House, shown in Plate 30 of *An Irish Florilegium vol 2* by Wendy Walsh (1983), by kind permission of the Walsh family
Right: Alderborough House (Raymond Daly)

. . . that a Geashill horticulturalist developed many varieties of the St Brigid Anemone?

The three-story towers at Fahy (outside Rhode, on the way to Edenderry) and Cloghan Beg (near Lusmagh) were windmills. A windshaft was mounted in a cap on top of each tower. Four canvas-covered sails harnessed the wind, turning the windshaft, which drove the millstones in the tower below.

The windmills probably shelled and ground oats for local people. Only seven windmills are known to have been built in Offaly, in places where watermills were not possible. Most of the county's windmills appear to have gone out of service by 1830, although the Fahy windmill may have been in use as late as 1880.

Left: Fahy Windmill (James Fraher)
Right: Cloghan Beg Windmill (Fred Hamond)

. . . that these towers once were windmills?

The earliest evidence for grey partridges in Ireland was found at an archaeological excavation at Newgrange dating to 2,500 BC. Before 1914, 21,000,000 grey partridge were shot and bagged annually across Europe. However, changes in farming practices, beginning in the 1970s, caused a population crash. In 2001, the recorded number of partridges in Ireland dropped to an all-time low of 22. Boora is the last known location of the wild grey partridge in Ireland.

With positive management by the Irish Grey Partridge Trust and the National Parks and Wildlife Service, the number of grey partridges had risen to 917 in 2013. This improvement has involved providing nesting cover, chick rearing cover, winter food crops and predator control.

Grey partridges live in family units called covies. The female lays 24 to 25 eggs, the largest known clutch of any bird. Each chick needs to eat 2,000 insects per day for the first three weeks after it hatches.

Left: Grey partridge (courtesy National Parks and Wildlife Service)
Right: Grey partridge (Eddie Dunne)

. . . that the last remaining population of the wild grey partridge in Ireland is at Boora?

HARRY CLARKE STAINED GLASS

Beginning in 1913, artistic genius Harry Clarke created intricate, gorgeous and sometimes bizarre stained glass windows for Irish churches. Today several Offaly churches feature Harry Clarke windows and windows by Clarke Studios, which continued Clarke's work after his death in 1931.

When the Catholic Church in Tullamore was rebuilt in the 1980s, the Jesuits donated several Harry Clarke windows from their retreat chapel at Rathfarnham Castle. The windows had been designed by Clarke and produced under his close supervision in 1927-28. Those of St Patrick and St Benignus received Clarke's particular attention.

In 1931, Clarke Studios provided five windows for the newly renovated St Manchan's Church in Boher. One shows the saint and his cow. St Mary's Church in Pollagh received a pair of Clarke Studio windows of the Virgin Mary and the Sacred Heart in 1936.

In 1931, 1941 and 1961 Clarke Studios installed seven windows in Mount St Joseph Abbey. The book *Lumen Christi,* published in 2009, tells the story those windows have played in the abbey's spiritual life.

The last religious institution in Offaly to receive Clarke Studio windows was Killina Convent Chapel near Rahan, which installed windows featuring Our Lady and the Resurrection in 1967.

Stained glass windows in Tullamore Catholic Church (James Fraher)

. . . that exquisite stained glass windows by Harry Clarke and by Clarke Studios adorn several Offaly churches?

Measuring just 8.75 m in length, the Molloy family home near Killurin is Offaly's smallest thatched house. Built in the 1800s, the house has many of the wonderful features of traditional Irish houses, including a hipped roof of oaten straw; thick, lime-washed stone and mud walls, a timber-battened half door and an open hearth.

Mrs Molloy's resourcefulness was legendary. Twice widowed, she raised her children in the tiny dwelling. She grew much of her family's food—including 'the finest rhubarb in Offaly'—as well as caring for cows, turkeys, pigs, hens, geese, guinea fowl and at least 10 cats.

Mrs Molloy whitewashed the house every Easter. Her son Paddy, a basketmaker, kept the thatch in good repair. Today the house at Killurin is lovingly maintained by Mrs Molloy's 14 grandchildren.

The Molloy's thatched house (James Fraher)

*. . . that Offaly's tiniest thatched house
is located near Killurin?*

One of the finest of Ireland's 25,000 masonry bridges is the arched bridge that spans the Silver River downstream of Cadamstown. Locally, it is known as the Ardara Bridge, after the old name for Deerpark townland.

The bridge was built near the medieval village of Cadamstown, which was burned in the 1640s and later rebuilt at its present location. When the Road Act of 1727 stipulated that all bridges be at least 12 feet (3.66 m) wide, many bridges were altered or replaced entirely. Although it measured just 9 feet (2.7 m) wide, the Ardara Bridge survived.

Local historian Paddy Heaney records that oak planks were put on top of the Ardara Bridge to make it 16 feet (4.88 m) wide so loads of turf and other carts could pass over it and on along the avenue to Cadamstown House.

The bridge can be viewed by walking the Offaly Way downstream from Cadamstown.

Ardara Bridge (courtesy National Monuments Service, Dept of Arts, Heritage and the Gaeltacht)

. . . that one of Ireland's finest old bridges spans the Silver River near Cadamstown?

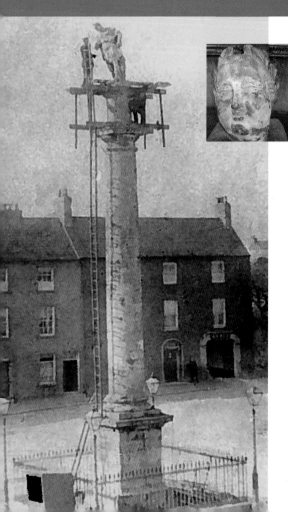

When he began to lay out the town of Birr in 1744, Sir Laurence Parsons of Birr Castle created what was then called Duke Square. The square's centrepiece was a column honouring the Duke of Cumberland, who was Prince William, the son of King George II. The square and column were completed in 1747, the year after the Duke defeated Bonnie Prince Charlie and his Scottish Highland Army at the Battle of Culloden.

To design the column, Sir Laurence employed a young Irish architect called Samuel Chearnley. He commissioned the leading sculptors of the day, John and Henry Cheere of Hyde Park in London, to make the Duke's statue.

Originally, the column stood within a circular enclosure, moated by a stream. It was paid for by subscription from the gentlemen of the region.

However, there is no Duke now! In 1915 the Town Council removed the statue from the column. Following the foundation of the Irish Free State in 1922, the square was renamed Emmet Square after Robert Emmet, the Irish Nationalist.

Left: The Duke being removed in 1915 (Offaly History)
Inset: The head of the Duke, now part of the Hunt Museum Collection
Right: The column before 1922 (Offaly History)
Far Right: The column today (James Fraher)

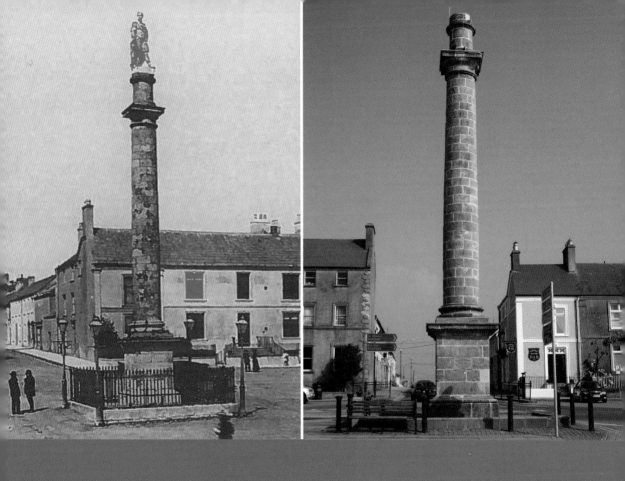

. . . that this is the first monumental column built in an Irish town?

It is not known if the Anglo-Normans introduced rabbits to Ireland, but the modern day Irish rabbit *(Oryctolagus cuniculus)* comes originally from southern Europe. In Ireland, the Anglo-Normans bred rabbits in a specially made rabbit-warren, which in Middle English was known as a *conynger*. In Irish, this word became *conicéar,* later anglicised into *coneyburrow*.

Just outside the town of Edenderry, there is a place still called Coneyburrow. This placename was recorded as early as 1550, when it was described in the Offaly Survey as *'the Connygere'*. The name is now incorporated in the name for a housing estate. There is another Coneyburrow recorded in Offaly: Coneyburrow Bridge in Castletown and Glinsk townland.

The name Coneyburrow serves as a reminder of the importance of rabbits as a source of food and fur in the farming economy of medieval Ireland. Rabbit-warrens were a significant asset on Anglo-Norman farming estates or manors. A rabbit-warren probably consisted of a mound of earth over an artificial series of tunnels, enclosed by a wall or an earthen bank with timber palisade or fence.

Top Left: Rabbit (Kevin Murphy)
Bottom Left: 1838 Ordnance Survey 6-inch Map
Right: A medieval rabbit warren illustrated in Psalm 100 of the Luttrell Psalter
(© The British Library Board; Add. 42130, f.176v)

. . . that around 840 years ago the Anglo-Normans farmed rabbits here?

In 2012, J.A.K. Dean calculated that 214 gate lodges once stood at the gates of Offaly's estates, which had as their focal points castles, houses and religious institutions. Today, just 102 survive. The people who lived in the gate lodges usually had responsibility for opening and closing the gates to the estate.

Often designed by the best architects of their day, gate lodges mirrored larger buildings in miniature, and occasionally whimsical, fashion. Some were small elegant Georgian structures. Others, like the gate lodges at Birr Castle, Kinnitty Castle and Charleville Forest, mimicked the architecture of medieval fortresses.

One quirky gate lodge, the Ink Pot outside Dunkerrin, was given its name by local people because of its peculiar circular roof, with a chimney at the centre. Eight children are said to have been reared within this tiny structure.

While many of Offaly's remaining gate lodges have been sealed and left empty, some are still used for holiday rentals or contain businesses. A number of gate lodges continue to be used as family homes but, because of their small size, they tend to have modern extensions.

Left top: The Ink Pot, Dunkerrin
Left bottom: Sharavogue gate lodge
Right: Clareen House gate lodge, Shinrone

. . . that 214 gate lodges once graced the entrances to Offaly's estates?

On the main road in Ballyboy village at the foothills of the Slieve Bloom Mountains is Dan and Molly's, the last pub in Offaly thatched with straw. Built before 1838, this pub has been re-thatched in the traditional Irish style, using oaten straw, every seven to 10 years since.

In April 2011, the roof of the pub caught fire. Fire brigades from Tullamore, Ferbane and Birr joined forces to quench the blaze. First they injected flame retardant foam into the roof. Once the blaze had been put out, firemen remained at the pub until 2:30 a.m., carefully removing a complete section of the surviving thatch by hand. As a result, 40 percent of the thatched roof was saved.

Just four months later, Dan and Molly's reopened. To this day it carries on tradition as a place for music, card games, sports analysis and general craic.

Dan and Molly's pub (James Fraher)

. . . that that this is the last pub in Offaly
thatched with traditional oaten straw?

Before 1977, archaeologists believed that Ireland's first people lived only near the coasts. Then bog harvesting at Lough Boora revealed what appeared to be an ancient stone road. An excavation led by Dr Michael Ryan of the National Museum found that the stony area was actually the storm shoreline of an ancient lake. The archaeological team also made a groundbreaking discovery: charcoal from campfires dating from 6,800-6,500 BC, a full 3,000 years before people were thought to have reached Ireland's interior.

Near the ancient campfires, archaeologists discovered more than 1,500 artefacts left behind by Mesolithic (Middle Stone Age) hunters. Many were carefully worked tools made from black chert, a flint-like stone. As well as cooking hearths, the site contained the remnants of ancient meals of wild pig, fowl, fish and hazelnuts.

Today nothing remains of the ancient encampment. However, beginning at the Boora Lake car park, a walk leads to the spot where thousands of years ago people stopped to eat and rest before continuing their hunt through the wilderness.

Left: Archaeologists on site in 1977, with kind permission of the National Museum of Ireland
Right: Boora today (Tom Egan)

. . . that this site changed our view of Irish history?

On Mullagh Hill, near Killurin, stands this tower. Located on the highest point of ground for miles around, it offers uninterrupted views of the surrounding countryside.

Around 1820, Rev Dr Francis Sadleir built the tower as a folly to ornament his property, Mullagh House. The tower has the unusual feature of a smaller turret on top and a spiral internal stone staircase.

A strong supporter of Catholic Emancipation, Sadleir was deeply concerned about the plight of the poor. In 1831 he became one of the first commissioners to administer funds used to educate disadvantaged children. In 1837, he was appointed Provost of Trinity College, a position he held until his death in 1851.

The house and formal grounds are long gone, but the folly tower remains.

Left: Rev Dr Francis Sadleir (Offaly History)
Right: The Tower on Mullagh Hill (Rachel McKenna)

*. . . that this whimsical tower was built
by a Provost of Trinity College?*

According to *Guinness World Records,* the box hedges at Birr Demesne are the tallest and oldest in the world. They stand about 10 m in height. Over 300 years old, they were part of the garden designed by Sir William Parsons in the mid-1600s. During World War I, some of the tall box on the demesne was cut down to make propellers and other parts for fighter planes.

More than 1000 plant species can be found in Birr Gardens; 50 of the garden's trees were featured in *Champion Trees of the British Isles* (Cornell University, 2009).

Box hedges (Birr Scientific and Heritage Foundation)

*. . . that Birr Demesne contains
the world's tallest box hedges?*

During the late 18th and early 19th centuries it was fashionable for owners to make their properties look ancient and historic. In many cases, they added the features that medieval castle owners had relied upon centuries earlier for defence.

When the architect Francis Johnston began to design Charleville Castle in conjunction with its owner, Charles William Bury, the 1st Earl of Charleville, defence had not been a major consideration for nearly 150 years. Yet the mansion, built between 1800 and 1812, incorporated gun loops and crenellations. Similar mock defensive features can be seen at Castle Bernard, also known as Kinnitty Castle, and also on the later phase of Birr Castle, which faces onto the demesne.

Since its construction, Charleville Castle, which is more correctly known as Charleville Forest, has been widely considered to be one of the finest Gothic houses in Ireland. In 1801 Lord Charleville wrote:

In truth I did not mean to make my House so Gothic as to exclude convenience and modern refinements in luxury. The design of the inside and outside are strictly ancient, but the decorations are modern.

Left: Charles William Bury, the 1st Earl of Charleville (Offaly History)
Right: Charleville Forest (Andy Mason)

*. . . that Charleville Forest is not a true castle
but a castellated mansion?*

These rocks were formed 350 million years ago at the end of the Devonian period of earth history. You can explore this site along the Silver River above Cadamstown where there is a Geological Nature Trail. Exposed in a cliff by the side of the river, you can see and examine a splendid section through the sandbars that formed in the channel of an ancient river (which was as big as the River Niger today and had a somewhat similar climatic setting), and the silt and mud that were washed onto the floodplain beside the river when it was in flood. These mudrocks are red in colour because all the iron in the sediment rusted in the hot climate that prevailed at the time.

The Silver River (Damien Egan)

. . . that in the Slieve Bloom mountains the Silver River slices into 350 million-year-old rocks?

For centuries, the rapids between Portumna and Banagher were a problem for those using the River Shannon to transport goods. Finally, around 1755, the Commissioners of Inland Navigation appointed engineer Thomas Omer to dig Clonaheenogue Canal. When completed, the 3.7 km-long canal bypassed the rapids at Meelick. At its southern end, Omer built Hamilton Lock, which was controlled by a lock keeper's house.

To accommodate large steamers, in the 1840s a second canal was dug under the direction of engineer Thomas Rhodes, who was employed by the Shannon Commissioners. Measuring just one km in length, the upgraded canal included the Victoria Lock.

Although the Clonaheenogue Canal and Hamilton Lock have long been abandoned, the second canal and Victoria Lock remain in use today.

Victoria Lock (James Fraher)

. . . that to avoid dangerous rapids, two canals were built along Offaly's stretch of the River Shannon?

LEMANAGHAN MONASTIC SITE

Visitors to the old monastic site at Lemanaghan are able to follow a stone flagged path (togher) that leads from St Manchan's Well and holy tree to a rectangular walled enclosure, called Kell. Within Kell, there is a small, one-roomed stone building, known as St Mella's Cell.

According to local legend, St Mella's Cell belonged to the mother of the monastery's founder. Tradition says that after St Manchan vowed never to speak to a woman again, he still met his mother, St Mella, every day on the stone togher. The two sat back to back, without speaking. According to legend, indentations in the togher's flags came from St Manchan's cow.

It may be that the stone togher was part of a network of wooden paths that led across the bog to the secluded monastic foundation. When St Manchan founded Lemanaghan on this spot in AD 645, one attraction was its isolation as an island of dry land surrounded by bog. Before long, however, a network of wooden walkways connected the monastery to the outside world. In 1997, a pilgrim's staff, incised with a Greek Cross and dating from the late 6th or early 7th century, was found beside one of these wooden walkways. It may have been lost by an early pilgrim to the monastery.

Left: The stone flagged path (James Fraher)
Right: Kell (James Fraher)

. . . that a stone flagged togher at Lemanaghan may have been the nexus of a network of ancient wooden walkways that crossed the bog?

Though they often go unnoticed, jostle stones like this one can be found at corners of buildings and entrance gates throughout Offaly. The stones kept carts and carriages from hitting and damaging buildings as they turned the corners.

Carved on this jostle stone is a bench mark: a broad arrow shape, pointing upwards, topped with a horizontal line. A surveyor carved a bench mark to provide a starting point for measuring altitudes in the surrounding area. By fixing an angle iron into the horizontal cut, the surveyor created a 'bench' onto which he or she could fit a levelling staff.

This practice gave rise to the expression 'bench mark': a fixed point from which other work can begin. Look out for other bench marks in the county. They can be seen on Blundell Aqueduct, Drumcooley milestone on the Grand Canal, Clonbulloge milestone, Cadamstown bridge, Feighery's Pub in Kilcormac, Birr Courthouse. . . .

Left: Jostle stone on the corner of Main Street and Church Lane in Birr (James Fraher)
Right: Bench mark (James Fraher)

. . . that this symbol is the origin of the term bench mark?

KINNITTY HIGH CROSS

In the grounds of Kinnitty Castle stands a fine 9th-century High Cross. As well as being decorated with three biblical scenes, it is inscribed to the memory of Maelsechnaill, who ruled the ancient kingdom of Meath from 846-862.

King of Meath? This makes no sense. If the monks at Kinnitty monastery had ever commissioned a high cross, surely they would have dedicated it to the King of Munster, rather than to his rival, the King of Meath. In ancient times, Kinnitty was on the Munster side of the provincial boundary, while Drumcullen was located in Meath.

Furthermore, the sandstone shaft and head of the cross at Kinnitty have been clumsily set into a limestone base. Obviously, the base and cross were not designed for each other.

The most likely explanation is that the Bernard Family, who lived at Kinnitty Castle, brought the cross from Drumcullen in the 19th century and made it a feature of their estate.

Left: Kinnitty Castle (James Fraher)
Right: Kinnitty High Cross (James Fraher)

. . . that the Kinnitty High Cross is most likely from the Drumcullen monastic site?

PAINTED LADY BUTTERFLIES

The Painted Lady is one of the most widely distributed of all butterflies, its range extending practically throughout the world except for South America and Australia. It needs a warm climate however, so it can only survive in Ireland during the summer. Its true home is on the edge of the deserts of North Africa, whence it crosses the Mediterranean into Spain when conditions become too hot in Africa, and then successive generations make their way further northwards across Europe, finally arriving in Ireland: sometimes in considerable numbers, in other years hardly any at all. It is possible that some individuals may fly from Morocco all the way to Ireland. It migrates at between 500 and 1,000 m high, thereby avoiding much wind turbulence.

The caterpillars usually feed on thistles (which explains the butterfly's scientific name, *Vanessa cardui: carduus* is the word for thistle in Latin; *Vanessa* means butterfly in Greek). The adults feed on the nectar of clovers, scabious, valerian, ivy and thistles. There may be several broods in Ireland, but the species cannot overwinter here, and all die with the advent of cold conditions in late autumn.

Left: Map of the Painted Lady's migration route from Morocco from the National Biodiversity Data Centre
Right: Painted Lady butterfly (Shutterstock)

*. . . that the Painted Lady butterfly comes to Offaly
all the way from Morocco?*

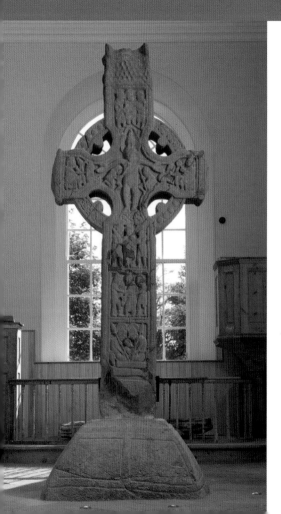

As well as founding many monasteries, including the great foundation at Durrow, Colum Cille was a gifted poet and scribe. While he was staying at the monastery of Droma Find (in Dromyn, County Louth), Colum Cille borrowed a book of Psalms from the monastery's founder, Finnian. Uncertain whether Finnian would allow him to copy the exquisite manuscript, Colum Cille made his own copy in secret. When he discovered what Colum Cille had done, Finnian was furious. He demanded that Colum Cille surrender his copy of the book. Colum Cille refused.

The two monks took the matter before Diarmait mac Cerball, High King of Tara. After hearing both sides of the case, Diarmait issued the following ruling:

To every cow its little cow, that is its calf, and to every book its little book [copy]; and because of that Colum Cille, the book you copied is Finnian's.

Left: Durrow High Cross today in St Columba's Church (James Fraher)
Right: St Columba's Church, Durrow (James Fraher)

. . . that the first copyright case involved Durrow's founding saint?

Underwater archaeological excavations during 1995-98 revealed the remains of a great wooden bridge in a shallow, narrow part of the River Shannon near the monastery of Clonmacnoise. Dating from AD 804, the bridge measured at least 120 m in length.

Master carpenters constructed the bridge by driving about 25 pairs of sharpened oak posts into the soft clay riverbed. Each post had an individual baseplate, made of beams and planks, to keep it from sinking further into the mud. The bridge's walking surface did not survive, but it could have been made of planks, poles or even woven hurdles.

Archaeologists also discovered 11 dugout boats near the bridge; three contained carpenters' axes and whetstones, lost when the boats sank.

Archaeologists found no evidence of reconstruction or repairs to the bridge. After 20 or 30 years of use, it appears that the structure fell into the water, where it remained undiscovered for nearly 1,200 years.

Left: A reconstruction of the early medieval bridge based on a modern aerial photograph (Conor McDermott, UCD School of Archaeology)
Right: Divers lifting one of the early medieval boats found in the river (Aidan O'Sullivan, UCD School of Archaeology)

. . . that Ireland's oldest known bridge crossed the River Shannon near Clonmacnoise?

Brown trout, known as croneen, are born and spend their early years in the Camcor River. As they mature, the trout swim downstream into the River Shannon and on to Lough Derg, where they spend most of their lives before returning to the headwaters of the Camcor to spawn.

After the Ice Age, when the rivers took on their modern arrangement as the glaciers finally melted, a particular population of trout, returning year after year to the sandy waters near the head of the Camcor, began to develop unique physical characteristics that will perhaps in the course of time make them sufficiently distinct to be considered a separate species.

Left: Silver River (Amanda Pedlow)
Right: Croneen (Eddie Dunne)

. . . that the Camcor River has its own distinctive brown trout?

The boundaries of County Offaly took a long time to create. In 1557, the Irish Parliament passed a law whereby the territories ruled by the O'Connors, known as Uí Fáilghe (Offaly) and Clanmaliere, ruled by the O'Dempseys, were formed into a new county, known as King's County. This area roughly comprises the present region of east Offaly.

Around 1570, the lands known as O'Molloy's Country in the central part of the county, along with those controlled by the MacCoghlans (part of west Offaly today) were taken from County Westmeath and joined onto King's County.

In 1591 the county boundaries were extended to include the region around Clara, known as Fox's Country. In 1606, at the request of Sir Mulroney O'Carroll, O'Carroll's Country was taken from County Tipperary and added to King's County.

The parishes of Harristown and Kilbracken, now in County Kildare, also formed part of King's County until the 19th century.

In about 1660, the parish of Lusmagh was taken from County Galway and added to King's County, thus completing County Offaly as we know it today.

Left: c.1561 Cotton Map (by kind permission of the British Library, Cotton MS Augustus 1, ii, 40)
Right: Map based on *A New History of Ireland, vol 9*, (1984)
Drawn by Catherine Martin

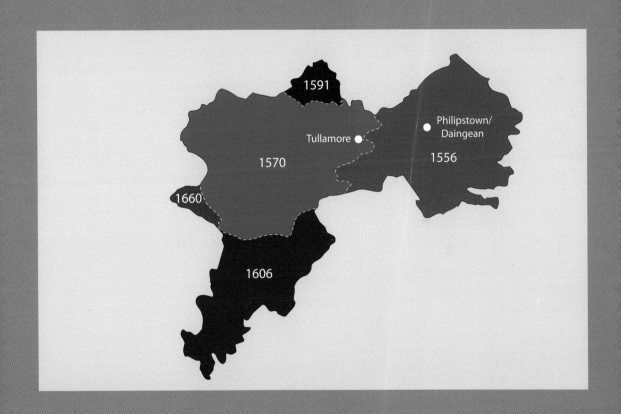

. . . that it took more than a century to piece together the boundaries of County Offaly?

WROUGHT IRON GATES

Before mass-produced goods became available, blacksmiths' skills were crucial to daily life. Blacksmiths were found throughout the county because every farmer needed to be able to get to a forge and back in the same day.

As well as making gates, blacksmiths maintained farm machinery, shod horses, shaped hoops for wheels and made essential tools for the home.

In England wooden gates were the norm, while wrought iron was popular in Ireland. Today, every gate made by an Offaly blacksmith bears witness to the distinctive craftsmanship of its maker. These unique gates should be treasured as local works of art.

Wrought iron gates (Shem Caulfield)

*. . . that unique wrought iron gates are
a feature of the county?*

In 1716, the Crown built a cavalry barracks in Tullamore, which was, at that time, a small town. The completed barracks accommodated 200 soldiers, their horses and equipment.

The barracks building was built in the shape of a 'star fort'. Its centre was a rectangle, with spear-shaped bastions jutting from each corner. The angles of the fort were ideal for mounting and firing artillery in case of attack. Most other star forts were built along the coasts; Charles Fort in Cork is a surviving example.

Troops remained at the fort in Tullamore until 1922, when the British Army departed. Shortly afterwards, Republican troops burned the building down.

Left: 1838 Ordnance Survey 6-inch Map
Right: The ruins of Tullamore's star fort (Amanda Pedlow)

. . . that just behind the Garda Station in Tullamore, there are the remains of an 18th-century 'star fort'?

St Mary's Church, Pollagh

Mindful of the distractions that can occur in mixed company, in 1907 Parish Priest Matthew Columb designed St Mary's Church in Pollagh to keep men and women apart. The finished building had two separate wings—one for men and one for women—that met at a central altar. Local people immediately christened the V-shaped building 'The Breeches Church'.

During renovations in 1959, architects bridged the gap between the two 'legs' of the church. The now fan-shaped building is known for its beautiful windows, installed by the Harry Clarke Studios in 1936, and its altar, chair and tabernacle of ancient bog yew, created by Michael Casey and the Celtic Roots Studio in 1991. To mark the church's centenary, a baptismal font and sanctuary lamp holder in bog yew were added to the altar furnishings.

St Mary's Church (James Fraher)

. . . that St Mary's in Pollagh was nicknamed
'The Breeches Church'?

In 1588 John Briscoe, a soldier in the army of Queen Elizabeth I, built a fine multi-storey tower house near what is now Tullamore. In its heyday the castle had gleaming, white-washed walls and a thatched roof. The castle featured many of the modern conveniences of its time: a murder hole over the front door, designed to discourage (permanently) unwanted guests and a loo on the second storey, which was connected by a chute to the exit hole on the outside at ground floor level.

During the 17th century, a house was built onto the castle. The line of its pointed roof can still be seen along one side of the castle's walls. Today both the original tower house and its later extension are ruins.

Left: Steps of Srah Castle (James Fraher)
Right: Srah Castle (James Fraher)

. . . that this is the oldest building in Tullamore?

COOLING TOWERS

On the 12th December 1999, more than 1000 people gathered outside the Power Station in Ferbane to watch as one of two cooling towers collapsed in a controlled explosion. It was a bittersweet moment for several onlookers, who had been present when the tower was constructed 42 years earlier.

For over 40 years, cooling towers were landmarks in the east of the county at Rhode and in the west at Lumcloon, Ferbane. The towers were built by the ESB in the 1950s and early 1960s as part of power stations that generated electricity with Bord na Móna milled peat. Standing 79-90 m high, the cooling towers transferred waste heat to the atmosphere. Following closure of the Ferbane Power Station, its cooling towers were demolished. Rhode Power Station closed shortly afterwards; demolition of its two towers occurred on the 16th March 2004.

Left: Dutch foreman Jan Thommissen with Irish Engineering & Harbour Construction Company Ltd and Michael Lonegan building the cooling tower for Ferbane Generating Station, 1956/7 (courtesy Eamon Dooley)
Right: The cooling towers at Lumcloon (James Fraher)

. . . that these cooling towers were famous landmarks in the Offaly landscape?

Before the days of hearses driving into cemeteries, it was usual for coffins to be carried to the graveyard on the shoulders of four or six men. The coffin rest was built by placing flat slabs on top of the graveyard wall flanked by a series of stone steps.

The coffin was placed on top of the flat surface for a short period of time before it was carried into the graveyard. In some instances this was the time when the coffin bearers were changed or the coffin was blessed or some other funeral custom was carried out. Coffin bearers were able to cross over the graveyard wall by using the stone steps on either side of the coffin rest.

The coffin rest at Roscomroe graveyard (Caimin O'Brien)

. . . that coffin rests were built into graveyard walls?

Shinrone Glass Furnace

During the years 1620-1660, Offaly was one of the main glassmaking centres of Ireland. Around this time, French Huguenot glassmakers, such as Phillip Bigoe and Annanias Hensey, came to the county where they constructed small glassmaking factories known as glasshouses. These glasshouses were located close to woodlands of oak and ash, which provided fuel for their glassmaking furnaces.

The wood-fired glass furnace at Glasshouse near the village of Shinrone is the only upstanding furnace in Ireland, Britain and France. Today the surface of the furnace interior glistens with the distinctive blue-green glass often described as 'forest-glass'.

Wood-fired glass furnaces were replaced by coal-fired glass factories in coastal ports, such as Dublin, Cork and the famous Waterford factory, bringing an end to the period when glass was made in Offaly.

Left: Shinrone glass furnace (Caimin O'Brien)
Right: Detail of Shinrone glass furnace (Caimin O'Brien)

*. . . that 390 years ago French families
were making window and vessel glass in Offaly
for the people of Dublin city?*

In September 2011, a hole a metre wide and four metres deep suddenly appeared near the top of Blundell Hill in Edenderry. Offaly County Council called on a team of geologists to investigate. Entering the opening in the ground, they concluded that it was a shaft leading to a failed silver mine, referred to as Blundell's Mine in several 19th-century accounts of the area. Pick marks on the walls of the shaft indicated that it had probably last been mined using the hand tools of the 1700s and 1800s.

Efforts to mine the hill for silver began in the mid-1700s. None were successful. By 1801, Sir Charles Coote recorded in the *Statistical Survey of the King's County* that '. . . on the Hill of Edenderry, now the churchyard, there was formerly a silver mine, twice attempted to be worked, but not within these forty years'.

Investigations into potential silver and lead mines have been conducted in the area as recently as the 1970s. So far, no mines near Edenderry have been economically viable.

Left: Exploring the shaft in 2011 (Amanda Pedlow)
Right: Geologist Martin Critchley in the mine (courtesy of Martin Critchley)

. . . that miners once sought silver
in Edenderry's Blundell Hill?

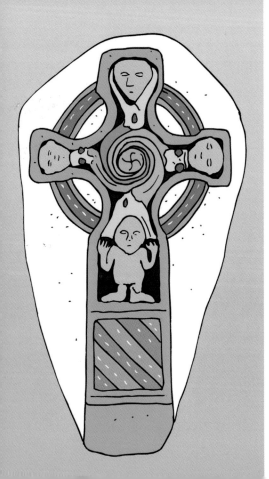

One of the carvings at the site of the early Christian monastery at Gallen shows a four-headed serpent slithering from a central whorl. Each of the serpent's heads grasps a human head in its jaws. At the bottom of this cross-shaped image a full human figure stands, hands uplifted.

The upright figure is in the *orans* position, a posture used for prayer during the Early Christian Period (400-1100).

On the Gallen slab, the four-headed serpent probably represents Evil. The four humans may symbolize the Evangelists, representatives of Good. The figure at the bottom of the image appears to convey the message that, by invoking the power of God through prayer, humankind will defeat Evil just as Christ did, through his death on the Cross.

More than 200 grave slabs were discovered during excavations at Gallen in the 1930s. Today a selection of those slabs can be viewed on a newly built wall on the site of the old church, or viewed as 3D scans on www.offaly.ie/heritage.

Left: A drawing by Paul Francis of what the carving may have looked like
Right: Gallen grave slab (James Fraher)

. . . that carvings on this grave slab probably represent the battle between Good and Evil?

IN MEMORY OF
THE OFFICERS
NON COMMISSIONED OFFICERS
AND MEN WHO SERVED IN
THE PRINCE OF WALES'S
LEINSTER REGIMENT
(ROYAL CANADIANS)
WHOSE HOME DEPOT WAS
HERE AT CRINKILL BARRACKS
1881–1922

THE LEINSTER

The threat of an invasion from France during the course of the Napoleonic Wars (1793-1815) led to the buildup of a large force in the midlands ready to repel an attack via the Shannon waterway. New barracks were built such as that at Crinkill near Birr, erected in 1809, while fortifications were also constructed at Shannonbridge and Banagher. As well as accommodating up to 2,000 men, Crinkill Barracks had its own church, hospital, gas works and sewerage system. Residents even had their own token money.

Securing the barracks adjacent to Birr was like a major industry coming to the town. For over one hundred years the military stationed at Crinkill had a significant impact on Birr's economic and social life. Crinkill Barracks was associated with the King's County Militia and the Leinster Regiment; the latter occupied one square of the barracks, while the second was occupied by visiting regiments.

Left: On the 21st September 2013, the Prince of Wales's Leinster Regiment (Royal Canadians) Regiment Association unveiled a memorial plinth at Crinkill Barracks to all those who served in this regiment (Rachel McKenna)
Right: The barracks was handed over to the Irish Free State in 1922, but was burned down shortly after by Republican forces; today nothing remains but sections of the fine perimeter walls and gates, along with the military cemetery (Rachel McKenna)

. . . that the large military barracks in Crinkill was built as a response to the Napoleonic Wars?

Sacred relics, the bones of St Manchan have stayed near his monastery since his death in 664. It is thought that around 1130, the metalworkers of Clonmacnoise created a shrine to house the bones.

For centuries, members of the Buckley family were guardians of the shrine. After the destruction of the church at Lemanaghan in the mid-1600s, they hid the shrine in a thatched school that served as a Penal Chapel. When that building burned down, the rescued shrine was placed in the safekeeping of the Mooney family. Soon the large number of visitors to the shrine led the Mooneys to place it with the Parish Priest at Boher.

In the 1800s, the shrine came to the attention of antiquarians, who displayed it at the Dublin Exhibition (1853), as well as exhibitions in London and Paris. Around that time, a buyer offered the people of Boher £400 for the shrine (a fortune at the time). They refused.

In June 2012, the shrine was stolen from the church at Boher. Thanks to the work of local garda, it was recovered in less than 24 hours.

Today, the Shrine of St Manchan (under increased security) is back at the church at Boher. Above it, a wonderful window by the Harry Clarke Studios depicts the saint, his cow and the extraordinary shrine.

St Manchan window and shrine (James Fraher)

*. . . that the relics of St Manchan have been venerated
for nearly 1350 years?*

From 1556 until 1920 Offaly was called King's County. The name was a tribute to King Philip II of Spain, who at that time was husband to Queen Mary, the last Roman Catholic monarch of England (1553-58). Laois became known as Queen's County.

Renamed Philipstown, also to honour King Philip, Daingean became the County Town. In 1835, Tullamore replaced Daingean as the County Town. After the foundation of the Irish Free State in 1920, King's County was renamed County Offaly and Philipstown reverted to Daingean.

Left: King Philip II of Spain by Titian, 1555, courtesy National Portrait Gallery London
Right: Philipstown (Daingean) as depicted on the 1838 Ordnance Survey 6-inch map

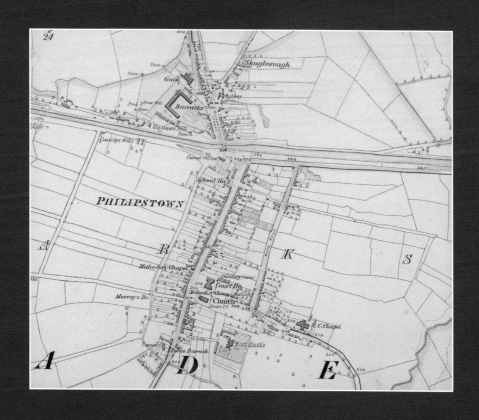

. . . that for 364 years Offaly was called King's County?

When the massive five-arch stone bridge at Belmont was built in the 18th century, it carried a road busy with carts and carriages. To accommodate those travelling by foot, the builders included pedestrian refuges where people could shelter safely while they waited for the traffic to pass by.

These were built on the upstream side of the bridge at road level where the piers project beyond the face of the bridge. At their bases are triangular cutwaters which serve to ease the flow of the passing water.

Today the refuges are ideal for viewing the River Brosna and the superb weir upstream. They are also a great place to watch kingfishers and Daubenton's bats in the summer evenings.

Left: Kingfisher (Andrew Howe)
Right: Belmont bridge refuge with the view upstream (Feargus McGarvey)

. . . that Belmont Bridge was built with walkers in mind?

Since 1974, parishioners and visitors to St Rynagh's Church in Banagher have been greeted by a colourful woodcarving by Imogen Stuart, an internationally acclaimed German-Irish artist.

In *The Madonna and Child*, the Virgin Mary stands on a crescent moon. In one of her arms, the Baby Jesus stretches out his arms to viewers. Four angels float on the other side.

The figures are presented against a mandorla: an almond shape created when perfect circles overlap. For some Christians this shape represents the coming together of Heaven and Earth.

In an interview, Stuart described the joyous spirit of her sculpture: 'She is there to comfort people, make them cheerful and smile. She is ethereal and floating in space and the nearby cherubs are there to underline the happiness of Mother and Child.'

The Madonna and Child by Imogen Stuart (James Fraher)

. . . that St Rynagh's Church in Banagher features Imogen Stuart's sculpture, The Madonna and Child*?*

A wonder housed within a treasure, the only copy of the 9th century *Gospels of Mac Regol* is on display inside Birr Library, which is located in a fine Gothic building designed by the renowned architect A.W. Pugin.

In the early 800s, when the monastery at Birr was at the height of its power, a scribe named Mac Regol wrote and illuminated the extraordinary manuscript. Although his images have been described as primitive, Mac Regol's brilliantly coloured book is recognized as a unique and important work of art.

By the 10th century, the book had made its way to England, where two monks added Anglo-Saxon text alongside its original Latin. Today the manuscript is part of the collection of the Bodleian Library at Oxford University.

Left: An illustration from the *Gospels of Mac Regol* (courtesy the Bodleian Library, University of Oxford. MS. Auct. D. 2. 19 Folio 127r)
Right: Birr Library (James Fraher)

. . . that the only copy of the Gospels of Mac Regol
can be found in this important historic building?

Rope Marks

The corners of Offaly's old limestone canal bridges often have deep, shiny grooves. These were worn by tow ropes attached to the horses that pulled the barges along the canal. The fastest barges were flyboats, pulled by four horses at a time, which could reach 16 km per hour, but actually averaged about 13 km per hour including time spent in locks.

The tow rope grooves and ridge marks are particularly clear at Shannonharbour bridge, but look for them on bridges all along the canal.

Left: Marks left by tow ropes on Shannonharbour bridge (James Fraher)
Right: Shannonharbour bridge (James Fraher)

. . . that the ropes pulling horse-drawn barges wore grooves into stone bridges?

An unusual item on display in Edenderry Library is a sheela-na-gig discovered in the Figile River in Kilcomber, between Edenderry and Clonbulloge.

No one knows the meaning of these haggard female figures, which display their genitals. Some people believe that they were originally fertility symbols. During the Medieval Period, many were set into the walls of churches, possibly to promote the moral teachings of the church. The fact that many were also built into the fabric of tower houses suggests that sheela-na-gigs were believed to ward off evil.

As of 2013, 111 sheela-na-gigs had been recorded in Ireland. In Offaly, a sheela-na-gig appears on the round window at St Carthage's Church of Ireland in Rahan; another, which was discovered close by, is now mounted inside the church. Other sheela-na-gigs in the county are on the tower houses at Garrycastle and Esker in Doon, and on the Nuns' Chapel at Clonmacnoise. Sheela-na-gigs from Birr and Seirkieran are part of the collection of the National Museum of Ireland.

Left: Figure on Chancel Arch, Nuns' Chapel, Clonmacnoise (James Fraher)
Right: Sheela-na-gig from the Figile River now in Edenderry Library
(Amanda Pedlow)

. . . that Edenderry Library has a sheela-na-gig on display?

In the mid-1600s, the Commonwealth forces were reported to be marching toward Ballyboy in the Parish of Kilcormac. As people frantically gathered their possessions, two women thought of the Pietà in the Parish Church. Quickly, they removed the statue and buried it in a pile of rubbish. Later, under the cover of darkness, a group of men buried the Pietà in a nearby bog.

In the early 1700s, the last person who knew the location of the Pietà was carried, on his deathbed, out to the bog. Under his direction, the statue was uncovered. It was in perfect condition.

Today the Pietà can be seen in the Church of the Nativity of the Blessed Virgin Mary in Kilcormac.

Left: The interior of Kilcormac church, painted in 1879 by William Johnson, shows the Pietà with a much stronger colour scheme than in the present day (Amanda Pedlow courtesy of Kilcormac Parish)
Right: Pietà (James Fraher)

... *that while the forces of the Commonwealth advanced through the midlands, the Pietà belonging to Kilcormac Parish was stashed safely in a bog?*

When a charismatic young priest, Father Andrew Mullen, died in 1818 at the age of 28, those who knew him were inconsolable. His mother cut his clothes into small pieces and gave them out as holy relics to all who believed in Father Mullen's goodness.

Not long afterwards, people began to make pilgrimages to Father Mullen's grave. One account, written in 1837, recorded that the grave had curative powers for those:

who frequently lie all night on the ground, under the tombstone, and mix milk, which they bring in a bottle, with the soil of the grave, and drink it. It is supposed to possess a miraculous power of healing and making whole. Many shreds of the garments of those who had visited the tomb, were hung upon small bent sticks at the foot of the grave, in commemoration of their having been cured.

Left: Father Mullen's grave in Killaderry near Daingean (Caimin O'Brien)
Right: Items left by believers at Father Mullen's grave (James Fraher)

*. . . that people have long sought cures
at Father Mullen's grave?*

The sea-lilies were creatures rather like sea-anemones, but with long stalks that anchored them to the sea floor. About 340 million years ago, forests of sea lilies thrived on the floor of a shallow tropical sea. These forests must have been there for thousands of years, because some of the beds of sea-lily limestone in the quarry located half-way between Shannonbridge and Clonmacnoise are a metre thick.

This Offaly quarry is the source of the famous Clorhane limestone. This rock was sometimes known as Clonmacnoise marble, although strictly speaking it is not marble (which is a metamorphic rock), but in Ireland limestone that could be polished was often called marble. It was in great demand in the 18th and 19th centuries for headstones and threshold stones. You can see these stones in many shops and other houses in towns like Birr, Ferbane and Tullamore—as well as further afield—but the most impressive example is the solid block of Clorhane limestone that is used in the counter of the Reception Area at the Visitor Centre at Clonmacnoise.

Left: Painting of the crinoid forest on the Lower Carboniferous sea floor (Jock Nichol, oil on canvas, 2011)
Right: Polished Clorhane limestone forming the counter at the Clonmacnoise Visitor Centre (Amanda Pedlow)

. . . that this is a kind of limestone made of fossilised sea lilies, which lived 340 million years ago?

VANITY FAIR.   April 5, 1873.

At the very beginning of his writing career, the great Victorian novelist Anthony Trollope (1815-82) lived in Banagher, where he worked for the General Post Office. From 1841-44, Trollope was assistant to the Post Office Surveyor for the west of Ireland, a job with extensive travel and opportunities for fox hunting.

While residing at the Shannon Hotel on Main Street in Banagher, Trollope wrote the initial draft of his first novel, *The MacDermots of Ballycloran,* based on the story of a bankrupt farming family. Three more of his 47 novels were set in Ireland. And though he is best-known today as a novelist, Trollope is also credited with a practical, if mundane, invention: the pillar postbox.

In 1970 the critic James Pope Hennessy took up residency in the Shannon Hotel while working on a biography of the great novelist. His book, *Anthony Trollope,* won the Whitbread Award for Biography in 1972.

Left: Illustration of Trollope, *Vanity Fair,* 1873 (Offaly History)
Right: Traffic passing the Shannon Hotel in the 1900s (G. Mallen, courtesy Offaly County Library Local Studies Collection)

*. . . that novelist Anthony Trollope
began his writing career in Banagher?*

CHARLOTTE BRONTË

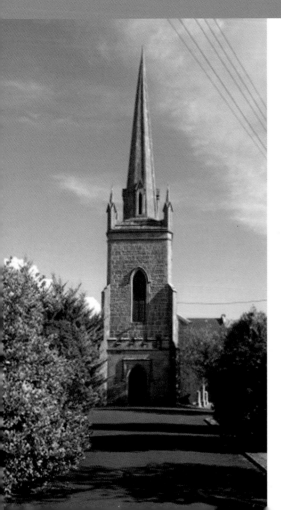

In 1854, Charlotte Brontë, the author of *Jane Eyre*, married the Reverend Arthur Bell Nicholls, who had been raised in Banagher by his uncle, Alan Bell, headmaster of the Royal Free School.

During their honeymoon in Ireland, the Reverend and Mrs Nicholls stayed at Cuba Court, Bell's residence just outside Banagher town. The novelist was struck by the beauty and tranquillity of the area, and by the esteem in which the local community held her new husband.

Unfortunately, their happy marriage was brief. While expecting her first child, Charlotte Brontë Nicholls contracted a fatal illness, possibly typhus or tuberculosis. She died in 1855.

Following his wife's death, Rev Nicholls continued as curate to her father, Rev Patrick Brontë, at Haworth, West Yorkshire. In 1861, he returned to Banagher, where he lived in Hill House until his death in 1906. He is buried in the graveyard of St Paul's Church of Ireland in Banagher.

Left: St Paul's Church of Ireland (Rachel McKenna)
Right: Hill House, now Charlotte's Way B&B (Amanda Pedlow)

. . . that Charlotte Brontë
was married to a Banagher man?

For hundreds of years, people relied on blacksmiths for essential tools and services. If a person could describe the implement he or she wanted, chances were that the smith could make it. As well as forging custom-made tools, cooking pots and other items, blacksmiths repaired machinery, made gates and shod horses.

There was a forge within a day's journey of every farm. Besides being workshops, forges were often the place where local people met up with each other for a chat while the blacksmith forged their goods. Large estates usually had their own blacksmiths.

In addition to blacksmiths, who forged hot iron or steel, there were also whitesmiths, who worked with cold, light-coloured metals, such as tin or pewter. They fashioned cups, pitchers, cutlery and candle holders. Sometimes whitesmiths did the final polishing and finish work on blacksmith-made items of iron or steel.

With mechanisation and mass-marketed goods, blacksmithing changed from an essential occupation into a craft.

Left: Whimsical horseshoe-shaped openings, complete with grooves and 'nail' markings, indicate that these 19th-century buildings were once blacksmiths' forges (Shem Caulfield)
Right: St Conleth's Forge, Daingean (Offaly History)

Forge. St. Conleths, Philipstown. Kings Co.

. . . *that for hundreds of years people 'shopped'*
at the forge of their local blacksmith?

Clonmacnoise Castle

In 1214 Anglo-Norman invaders built a castle at an important crossing point on the River Shannon to help secure their territory. At the time, this site was part of an orchard belonging to the monastery.

Two years later, King John of England paid compensation to the Bishop of Clonmacnoise for 'his land occupied in fortifying the castle of Clonmacnois, for his fruit trees cut down, his cows, horses, oxen and household utensils taken away'.

The castle appears to have been abandoned during the 1300s, when there was an upsurge in the power of local Gaelic kings.

Clonmacnoise Castle (James Fraher)

. . . that Anglo-Norman invaders paid compensation to the Bishop of Clonmacnoise after they built a castle in his orchard?

FISH WEIRS

When the water levels are low, you can see the remnants of stone-built eel weirs at Shannonbridge. In earlier times, these V-shaped ramparts of large, loose stones funnelled water containing eels and other fish into wooden cages or baskets. Eels were also abundant in the Brosna callows before they were drained in the late 19th century, and the remains of several eel weirs can still be seen along that river too.

During medieval times, and probably earlier, fish caught in weirs were food for the rich and powerful. In 1185, Giraldus Cambrensis wrote that the River Shannon 'abounds in lampreys, a dangerous delicacy indulged in by the wealthy'. In 1622 there are historical references to the *'Great Wear of Raghra'* (now Shannonbridge), which, along with several other weirs on the River Shannon, was included in the fishing rights of Raghra Castle.

Immediately after hatching in the southern Sargasso Sea, European eels *(Anguilla anguilla)* journey nearly 5,000 km towards Europe, where they dwell in rivers and lakes for 10-30 years. When they are ready to spawn, mature eels travel back to the Sargasso Sea. It was during this return journey that adult eels were trapped in weirs.

Left: Map showing eel-weirs at Shannonbridge (National Archives of Ireland (NAI), Ordnance Survey, Fair Plan, King's County – OS 105/C, sheet 244)
Right: A lamprey (courtesy National Parks and Wildlife Service)

. . . that eels and lampreys were once a delicacy enjoyed by the elite?

In the graveyard at Gallen, Ferbane, a beautifully carved headstone marks the burial place of blacksmith Thomas O'Connor, who died in 1799. Above the inscription, the stonecarver has depicted the tools of Mr O'Connor's trade, including his bellows, anvil and hammer.

In the graveyard at St Carthage's Church in Rahan is the elaborately carved headstone of John Flanagan, who died on the 7th January, 1775. It is decorated with the Crucifixion, humanoid images of the Sun and Moon and, in a horizontal band across the headstone, the tools he used as a carpenter. These include a saw, hammer and dividers.

Tradesmen's headstones decorated with tools of their trade, as well as religious imagery, offer a fuller picture of the person's life on Earth.

Left Top: The symbols on John Flanagan's headstone, Rahan (Caimin O'Brien)
Left Bottom: The inscription on John Flanagan's headstone, Rahan (Offaly History)
Right: Thomas O'Connor's headstone, Gallen (James Fraher)

. . . that a number of Offaly headstones feature carvings of tradesmen's tools?

WAR DEPARTMENT BOUNDARY STONES

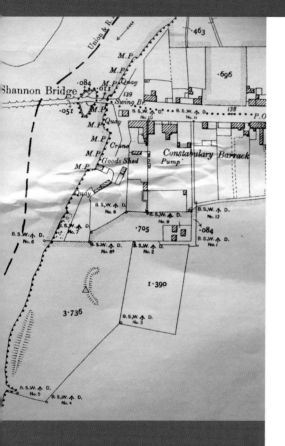

To secure the River Shannon during the Napoleonic Wars (1793-1815), the Board of Ordnance constructed the military barracks at Shannonbridge. The 25-inch Ordnance Survey map of 1910 depicts twelve points enclosing the military property belonging to the barracks that are labelled B. S. W. ↑ D. No. 1 to No. 12. The letters annotated on the map stand for Boundary Stone War Department (later renamed the Ministry of Defence).

The upward pointing arrow is a symbol known as the 'Broad Arrow' which identifies this land as government property belonging to the Board of Ordnance. On the ground there is a small upright boundary stone at each location marked on the map. The top of each boundary stone is inscribed with the letters W ↑ D standing for War Department or B ↑ O meaning Board of Ordnance with a number beneath. Beginning at the east and running in a clockwise direction, the stones are numbered 1 to 12.

Left: 1910 Ordnance Survey 25-inch map showing the location of the boundary stones
Right: Boundary stones (Caimin O'Brien)

. . . that 12 carved stones delineated the boundaries of the military barracks at Shannonbridge?

One May morning in 2003, a local man, Kevin Barry, was working with a digger on the bog just below Croghan Hill. When he discovered part of a human body, he phoned the garda. However, it soon became clear that even if the corpse had been a victim of foul play, arrests would be impossible. The body was more than 2,000 years old.

While several prehistoric bodies have been found in bogs in Ireland and and more widely in Northern Europe, 'Old Croghan Man' was unique in a number of respects. For one thing, he was very tall. Specialists estimate that he may have stood 6 ft 6 in, and would have been in his twenties.

The well-manicured hands of Old Croghan Man indicate that he was not a manual labourer and, very likely, was of noble birth or held a privileged status in his society. In fact, the bog had preserved his body so perfectly that a member of the garda was able to take his fingerprints— possibly the oldest on record in Ireland.

Only the torso, arms and hands of Old Croghan Man have been discovered. They bear signs of torture and mutilation. Experts have concluded that three to four centuries before the birth of Christ, Old Croghan Man was killed as a human sacrifice. Today his body is on display in the Kingship and Sacrifice exhibition at the National Museum of Ireland in Dublin.

*. . . that a famous bog body was discovered
near Croghan Hill?*

No one knows what led builder Michael Hayes to abandon the modest dimensions of a standard lock-keeper's house when he built the 26th lock house near Tullamore in 1800. The resulting structure has three storeys at the rear and two facing the canal. Unlike the usual rectangular lock houses, it is oval in shape, with a curved bow on one side and a castellated projecting porch on the other.

Unimpressed, the directors of the Grand Canal Company refused to meet 'the extraordinary and unnecessary' extra expense of £42.17s.7d sought by Hayes for the design and construction of the lock keeper's house. Today, however, the protected structure is a treasure. It is known as Boland's Lock Keeper's house, after the last family of lock keepers who lived here.

Left: Boland's Lock Keeper's house (Offaly History)
Right: The view of the house from the 26th Lock (James Fraher)

. . . that Boland's Lock Keeper's House was way over budget?

Around 10,000 years ago, just at the end of the Ice Age, these boulders stood at the edge of the extensive network of lakes that dominated the landscape of Offaly. They were just ordinary boulders to start with; they acquired their fantastic shapes as a result of the long-continued lapping action of waves breaking on the shore.

Many hundreds of years after the Ice Age, the water level of the lakes dropped, leaving these lake-edge marker stones stranded. Today we can use the stones to help plot the extent of lakes in the early post-glacial period, when the first people arrived in Offaly and began to camp along the lake shores.

Left: Ballylin stone (Louise Dunne)
Right: Clonkeen stone (Louise Dunne)

. . . that limestone boulders resembling enormous mushrooms or modernist sculptures mark the shorelines of long-lost ancient lakes?

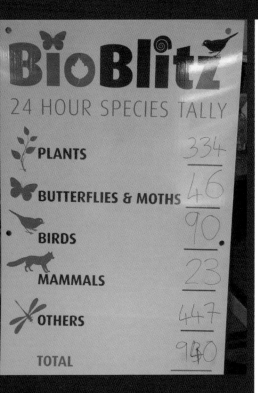

At 5 p.m. on Friday 18th May 2012, 50 wildlife experts gathered at Lough Boora Parklands. Their mission: to record each and every living thing they could find at the midlands site within 24 hours. By 5 p.m. the next day, they had counted 940 different species, including 90 birds, 334 vascular plants, 23 mammals, 52 lichens and 90 mosses and liverworts.

Boora was the first midlands site selected to participate in the Bioblitz organized by the National Biodiversity Data Centre. The results proved that, just two decades after peat harvesting ceased at Boora, a wide variety of wildlife has re-colonised the cutaway.

Left: The totals for the day (Amanda Pedlow)
Right: George Smith, bryophyte recorder at work (Amanda Pedlow)

. . . that 940 species were recorded in just 24 hours during the Boora Bioblitz?

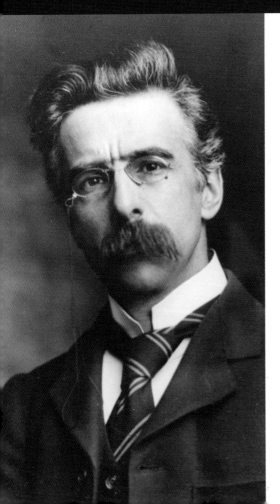

For nearly 50 years, John Joly made astounding breakthroughs in a variety of scientific fields.

Born in the Church of Ireland Rectory near Bracknagh in 1857, Joly spent his entire career at Trinity College, Dublin.

Early on, he invented three ground-breaking devices: the meldometer, which measures the melting points of minerals; the steam calorimeter, which measures heat outputs, and the photometer, which measures the intensity of light.

Joly went on to pioneer the first reliable method of printing colour photographs from a single plate. After inventing a new way to extract radium, Joly collaborated on methods to use both radium and radon gas to treat tumors in cancer patients.

During his legendary academic career, Joly authored more than 270 scientific papers. His wide-ranging topics included the sap rising in plants, the age of the Earth and continental drift.

Trinity students loved him for his work running the film and photography society, as well as his knowledge in music, art and—late in life—motorcycles.

Left: Portrait of John Joly (courtesy of Trinity College, Dublin)
Right: Joly's birthplace, Hollywood House, near Bracknagh by kind permission of the owners (Amanda Pedlow)

. . . that Offaly-born inventor John Joly was an extraordinary all-round scientist?

Two carved faces showing the elaborate facial hair styles of Irish noblemen appear on the 12th-century chancel arch at St Carthage's Church in Rahan. However, moustaches like these were outlawed in Ireland—at least for Englishmen—for well over a century.

In 1447, at Trim, Co. Meath, an Act of Parliament was passed in an attempt to distinguish between Englishmen living in Ireland and the native Irish. The Act stated that 'an Englishman shall not use a beard upon his upper lip alone, and that the said lip shall be once shaved, at least in every two weeks; the offender to be treated as an Irish enemy'. This Act was repealed in 1635.

In 1539 Henry VIII passed a law which made it illegal for any subject in Ireland to 'have or use any haire growing on their upper lippes, called or named a cronmeal'. The Act also stated that no person in Ireland 'shall be shorn or shaven above the ears, or use the wearing of haire upon their heads like unto long lockes, called glibbes'.

St Carthage's Church, Rahan (James Fraher)

. . . that in 1447 it was illegal for an Englishman living in Ireland to sport a moustache?

There are 35 km² of callows between Athlone and Portumna and about half are in Co. Offaly. The gradient of the river is infinitesimal—about 2 cm every kilometre—which is why it overspills onto the callows so often.

The callows are used as pasture and hay meadow in summer and are owned by over 600 farmers.

There are a total of 33 species of grasses, 31 species of sedges and ten species of orchids among the 220 or so native plant species that make up these natural floodplain grasslands, supporting around 30 types of breeding birds and innumerable insect species.

Hay meadows on natural grasslands are rare in Europe; impressively, Co. Offaly has an estimated 400 ha of hay meadows on its callows.

In winter, the callows are regularly home to the largest inland concentration of birds in Ireland, totalling 30,000 or so. Up to 23 species of ducks, geese and wading birds migrate from frozen latitudes as far apart as Greenland and Siberia to find food and refuge on the callows.

Left: About 4,000 Black-tailed Godwits, one-tenth of the entire world population, winter on the Shannon Callows each year (Mark Carmody)
Right: Wild flowers on the callows (Stephen Heery)

. . . that the Shannon Callows offer food and refuge to native plants, birds and insects?

GLENREGAN LIME KILN

Reaching an internal temperature of 900°C-1100°C, lime kilns like this one burned limestone as part of the lime making process. When people added water to the burnt limestone, it changed into a powder, known as slaked or hydrated lime, that was used for many purposes.

Builders used lime in their mortar to bind the stones of a wall together. People constructing traditional buildings covered both the internal and external faces of walls with lime plaster of various colours. A lime mortar, traditionally referred to as a 'dash' was used to cover external walls; this process was known as 'dashing'.

Over the last 100 years, lime mortar has gradually been replaced by concrete. Farmers commonly add lime to the soil as a fertiliser. As well as reducing the acidity of the soil, 'liming' helps to break down heavy clay soils, making the land more fertile.

Left: Lime wash on a farmhouse in the townland of Castletown and Glinsk, adjacent to Glenregan (Caimin O'Brien)
Right: Glenregan lime kiln (Amanda Pedlow)

. . . that this structure once burned stone
as part of the lime-making process?

The Offaly County Crest features bog rosemary, a wildflower found in midland bogs and rarely seen elsewhere in Ireland. This plant grows by bog pools, among sphagnum moss and on areas recently burnt.

The great Swedish botanist Linnaeus was extremely taken by bog rosemary when he encountered it in the bogs of Lapland. He gave the plant its scientific name, *Andromeda polifolia*, after the princess Andromeda in Greek mythology. In the myth, Andromeda's mother boasted that her daughter was more beautiful than the sea nymphs. This infuriated Neptune, who ordered that the princess be chained to a rock as a sacrifice to sea monsters. At the last minute, Perseus rescued Andromeda and eventually made her his wife.

When he first saw the gorgeous drooping pink flowers of bog rosemary, surrounded by wetland pools filled with 'poisonous dragons and beasts—i.e. evil toads and frogs', Linnaeus thought of Andromeda, her head bent in despair and pink cheeks fading with fear, chained to a rocky island surrounded by dark and dangerous waters.

Right: Bog rosemary (Fiona Feehan)

. . . that the Offaly County Crest features an unusual wildflower of the midlands?

PIGEON HOUSES

Once used to raise pigeons for food, this circular roofless tower stands on the corner of the courtyard wall of the 17th-century dwelling known today as Hollow House.

Inside the pigeon house, several tiers of small nest-holes were placed high above the ground, to make it more difficult for rodents to kill the young pigeons. Most of the nest-holes have square-shaped openings. Inside the thick walls, each one turns in at a right angle, making an L-shape. Inside this dark and secluded space, the pigeons built nests and raised squabs: young, unfledged pigeons, which were a valuable source of food for the country house.

The 'house-pigeons' belonged to the occupants of the adjoining house and were protected by law. The mere presence of a pigeon house was proof of the high status of the owners.

House-pigeons were considered domestic fowl rather than wild game. During the first half of the 19th century the unlawful taking or killing of such birds was punishable by a fixed penalty not exceeding 40 shillings.

Hollow House, Tinnycross near Tullamore (Caimin O'Brien)

. . . that this circular tower once housed nesting pigeons?

When Charles William Bury began to build a mansion outside Tullamore in 1801, a giant oak tree dominated his property 'like a watch tower'. Today the King Oak, one of Ireland's finest and oldest surviving native trees, continues to stand guard at the entrance of Charleville Demesne. Estimates of its age range from 400 to 900 years. The massive oak measures 7.9 m around at its widest point. Four of its branches touch the ground; the longest measures 23 m from trunk to tip.

The King Oak is part of the country's largest surviving forest of native oaks, a remnant of the great forests of *Quercus robur.*

In deference to the fine oaks on his land, Bury named his completed mansion Charleville Forest. Over time, the Burys came to believe that if a branch of the King Oak fell, one of their family would die. To prevent that from occurring, they used wooden props to shore up the tree's great branches. When a thunderbolt struck the King Oak in May 1963, the tree survived. However, the head of the family, Colonel Charles Howard-Bury (famous for climbing Mount Everest) passed away in September of that year.

King Oak (Rachel McKenna)

. . . that one of Ireland's most extraordinary trees stands in Charleville Demesne?

St Ciarán's Bush

People of faith have long tied rags to a special hawthorn bush near the old monastery of Seirkieran, in Clareen. A stone at the base of the rag bush is said to bear the imprint of St Ciarán's hands and knees.

On the 5th March, the saint's feastday, pilgrims attend mass, go to the well, then pause at the bush before going on to the graveyard.

According to tradition, when travelling past the bush, the bush must always be passed on the left side; to do otherwise would invite bad luck.

St Ciarán's Bush (James Fraher)

. . . that for centuries St Ciarán's Bush has been treasured as one of Offaly's rag trees?

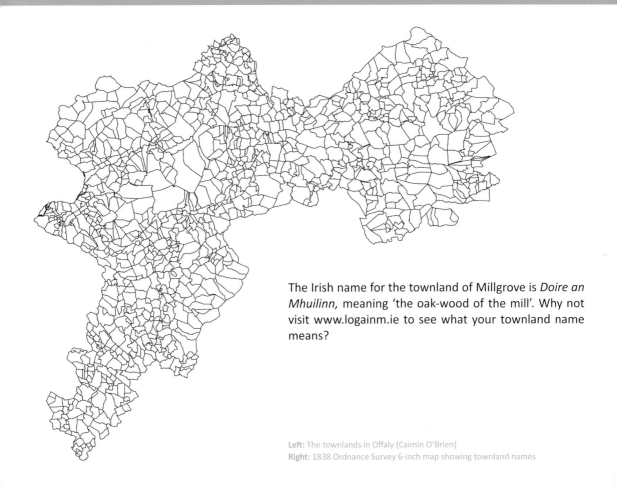

The Irish name for the townland of Millgrove is *Doire an Mhuilinn,* meaning 'the oak-wood of the mill'. Why not visit www.logainm.ie to see what your townland name means?

Left: The townlands in Offaly (Caimin O'Brien)
Right: 1838 Ordnance Survey 6-inch map showing townland names

. . . that Offaly has 1,148 townlands?

Many of the buildings surrounding the triangular green in Geashill date from the 1860s and 1870s, when the landlord, Lord Digby, set out to improve the village.

In 1837, Geashill consisted of about 87 thatched houses. Not long after, many of them were described as 'modern ruins'. Using the workers' cottages on his estate in Dorset as a model, Lord Digby replaced many of the thatched, mud-walled buildings with slate-roofed, stone houses. The new dwellings featured larger windows and sandstone-flagged floors.

Lord Digby's improvements won international acclaim. At the Paris Exhibition of 1867 he was awarded the bronze medal for models of his cottages in Geashill. The Royal Agricultural Society awarded him gold medals over three consecutive years for improving the greatest number of cottages in the best manner in the province of Leinster. Not only were the cottages warm and practical, the Society wrote, but 'every recess was made available, either by shelves, cupboards, or boxes for the use and convenience of the inhabitants'.

Today many of the award-winning cottages continue to be used as family homes, a tribute to their good design.

Geashill cottages (Rachel McKenna)

. . . that Geashill's 19th-century cottages won international awards for design?

As motorists drive along the Tullamore bypass, they are greeted by *Saints and Scholars,* four 7.5-m-high sculptured steel figures, each standing on its own gravel hill. One holds a book aloft. Another raises a chalice. A third grasps a staff. From the outstretched hands of the final figure, a flock of birds rises to the heavens. Illuminated manuscripts inspired the patterns on the sculptures.

The sculptures stand looking out over the place where the modern bypass cuts through the Eiscir Riada, a snakelike gravel ridge that was the route for pilgrims travelling west towards Clonmacnoise.

Artist Maurice Harron created the statues in 2008. He is also the sculptor of *The Gaelic Chieftain,* which overlooks a battle site in the Curlew Mountains in County Roscommon.

Left: *The Gaelic Chieftain* by Maurice Harron (James Fraher)
Right: *Saints and Scholars* by Maurice Harron (James Fraher)

. . . that four sculptures on the Tullamore bypass honour Offaly's early Christian monasteries?

During one of the bleakest periods in the Irish history, Falmouth Kearney, the 19-year-old son of a Moneygall shoemaker, left his home and travelled to Cork. Boarding the SS Marmion in 1850, he sailed to America to begin a new life.

Nearly 161 years later, Kearney's great-great grandson returned to Offaly. Despite concerns about a cloud of volcanic ash over Iceland, he boarded Air Force One in Washington DC. After landing in Dublin, he journeyed on by helicopter, eventually rolling into Moneygall on the 23rd May 2011 in an armoured vehicle called The Beast.

Amid driving showers and strong sunshine, President Barack Hussein Obama and his wife Michelle greeted well-wishers for nearly an hour. Before continuing their journey, the couple retired, briefly, to Ollie Hayes' pub.

The president insisted on paying for his pint.

Left: President Obama's ancestral home in Main Street, Moneygall (Amanda Pedlow)
Right: The President and First Lady In Moneygall (Andrew Murray)

. . . that a U.S. president is descended from a Moneygall shoemaker?

The woollen dress, known as the Shinrone Gown, is now part of the collection of the National Museum of Ireland.

A similar gown was described in the 1620s by Luke Gernon, who wrote:

[they] have straight bodies, and long waists, but their bodies come no closer but to the middle of the ribs, the rest is supplied with lacing, from the top of their breasts, to the bottom of their placket [opening in the upper part of a skirt], the ordinary sort have only their smocks [shirt-like undergarment] between, but the better sort have a silk scarf about their neck, which they spread and pin over their breasts. They have hanging sleeves, very narrow, but no arming sleeves, other than their smock sleeves, or a waistcoat of stripped stuffe, only they have a wrestband of the same cloth, and a list of the same to join it to their wing, but no thing on the hinder part of the arm least they should wear out their elbows. The better sort have sleeves of satin. The skirt is a piece of rare artifice.

Clothing historian Kass McGann studied the gown in the National Museum and made this dress as a reconstruction (© Kass McGann, ReconstructingHistory.com)
Images of original gown reproduced with kind permission of the National Museum of Ireland

. . . that in 1843 a 400-year-old dress was discovered in Shinrone bog?

Tiger Beetle

If the tiger beetle were 100 times bigger, it would deter even the bravest of us from ever setting foot on the bog. The adult beetle is like an iridescent emerald jewel. However its ferocious larva lives in a vertical burrow in the bare peat, where it lies in wait for prey, using its thorax as a camouflaged 'manhole'. When an unsuspecting insect comes close enough, the larva does a somersault that catapults the unfortunate creature into the shaft, where it is devoured.

Top Left: Tiger beetle (John Feehan)
Botton Left: Cutaway bog (Tom Egan)
Right: Close up of tiger beetle (Barry Cregg)

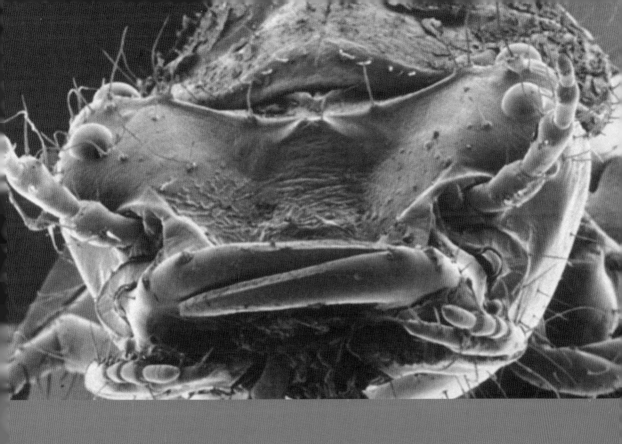

. . . that cutaway bog is the favourite habitat of the tiger beetle?

People living in Geashill and the surrounding area often enjoy a stroll along the Glebe Walk. This pathway, framed by beech trees, extends from the Cottage out to the Tullamore Road. Along the way, it is not unusual to see native red squirrels, as well as dozens of wildflowers.

In earlier times, this tree-lined walkway was an avenue leading to the Glebe House, later known as the Rectory, which was the residence of the rector of St Mary's Church. The path cuts through the Glebe, a parcel of land which was used to support a parish's priest or rector.

At Geashill, the Glebe was substantial. Samuel Lewis, in 1837, wrote that Geashill had two glebes comprising 82 acres. By 1841, the Glebe at Geashill had grown to 91 acres. Around 1900, Geashill's Rectory was surrounded by formal gardens and amenities, including a fish pond and an ice house. The house was demolished in the 1960s but the walk remains.

Left: The Glebe Walk (Rachel McKenna)
Right: The Rectory (Offaly History)

. . . that Geashill's Glebe Walk once led to the Rectory?

Despite resistance from the Railway Company, which saw few potential profits in such a venture, the local gentry, in conjunction with the Parish Priest in Ferbane, pushed through formation of the Clara & Banagher Railway. After raising funds through a charge on the Local Rates for the Barony of Garrycastle, the Clara & Banagher Railway opened on the 29th May 1884.

The line was just 32 km in length. It served stations at Ferbane, Belmont and Banagher. As well as carrying passengers, the Clara & Banagher Railway had a Goods Service, including special wagons for carrying cattle. The Passenger Service ended in 1947, although afterwards provision was made for people on their way to matches in Dublin, trips to the sea in Galway or on pilgrimage to Knock.

At the end of its 78 years in operation, the Clara & Banagher Railway proved the original reservations of the Railway Company correct: it was never profitable. After the line closed for good on the 1st January 1963, its rails were lifted. Other railway lines in County Offaly included Enfield/Edenderry (1877-1963), Birr/Roscrea (1858-1963), Streamstown/Clara (1863-1947) and the Portarlington/Athlone line, which is the only one that remains in operation.

Left: Stile and gate near Lemanaghan on the old railway line (Amanda Pedlow)
Right: Banagher Railway Station (courtesy of Kieran Keenaghan)

. . . that a railway line once ran from Clara to Banagher?

BLUNDELL AQUEDUCT

While dozens of roads cross over the Grand Canal, there is only one place in Offaly where the reverse is true. By building up the canal's banks on top of the bog, the Grand Canal Company constructed the Blundell Aqueduct to carry the Grand Canal over the Edenderry-Rathangan Road. This structure is the only water-over-road bridge in the county.

Named for the Blundell family of Edenderry, the aqueduct was completed in 1793, well in advance of the rest of the Grand Canal, which opened in 1797.

Left: Blundell Aqueduct (Amanda Pedlow)
Right: National Archives of Ireland (NAI), Ordnance Survey, Fair Plan, King's County – OS 105/C, sheet 225

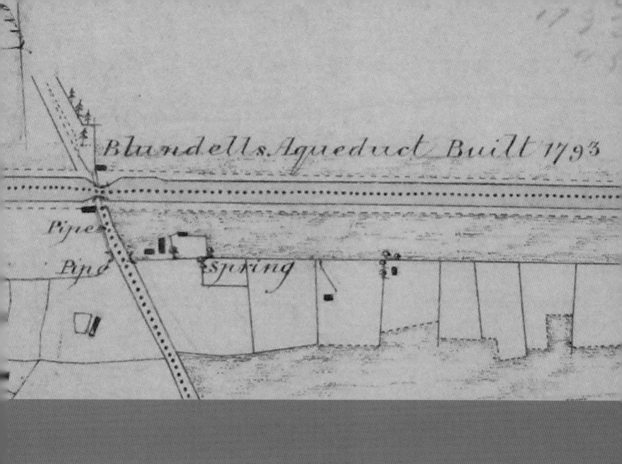

. . . that this bridge is actually an aqueduct?

In the centre of Market Square in Birr is a statue of the Maid of Erin with the symbols of the cross, harp and wolfhound. It commemorates one of the notable episodes of the Fenian movement in which three Irish Nationalists—Michael O'Brien, William Philip Allen, and Michael Larkin (who came from Lusmagh)—were executed in Manchester in 1867. The three men were convicted for the shooting of a police sergeant during the rescue of Colonel Kelly and Captain Deasy, two leaders of the Irish Republican Brotherhood, as they were being conveyed to Salford Gaol, near Manchester.

The monument was unveiled by O'Donovan Rossa in 1894. The photo on the right is from the Mason Collection in the National Library showing the unveiling of the monument.

A newspaper report from 1968 tells us that it was only on St Patrick's Day in that year that the plaques with the names, date and place of execution were added, rectifying this 'peculiar omission' in 1894.

Left: *Maid of Erin* (James Fraher)
Right: The unveiling of the monument in 1894 (courtesy of the National Library of Ireland; M20/29/2)

*. . . that this monument commemorates
three Irish Nationalists?*

When St Ciarán died less than a year after founding Clonmacnoise, the parallels between his life and that of Jesus Christ did not go unnoticed. Both were the humbly born sons of carpenters who died at age 33. Almost immediately, the devout began to make the journey to Ciarán's tomb.

In the first recorded incidence of pilgrimage in Ireland, the *Annals of Tigernach* state that in 606, Aedh, an Irish chief, died on his way to Clonmacnoise. Thousands of other pilgrims made the same journey. Many travelled along the Eiscir Riada, a chain of eskers: dry, well-drained ridges created by melting glaciers during the last Ice Age.

For pilgrims the esker route was dry underfoot and afforded a view over the surrounding countryside. Today a signed cycle route from Ballycumber to Clonmacnoise travels along this ancient pilgrimage road.

Left: Pilgrims' Road (James Fraher)
Right: Clonmacnoise (James Fraher)

. . . that an ancient Pilgrims' Road leads to Clonmacnoise?

On the 1st April 1888, opposite the County Arms Hotel in Birr, Sarsfields of Thurles (representing Tipperary) met the Meelick Club of Galway in the first ever All-Ireland Hurling Final. Birr was chosen to host the match because even in 1888 it had a well-established hurling tradition. Also it was the most central town between the two opponents. In the end, scoring 1-1 to Meelick's 0-0, Tipperary won the match.

On the 125th anniversary of the GAA, Offaly hurling star Brian Whelahan and GAA President Christy Cooney unveiled a 3.3-m-high statue commemorating that first All-Ireland match. The sculpture by Mayo-based artist Mark Rhode is shown wearing the clothes and wielding a hurl of the type used in the 19th century.

Mark Rhode's sculpture in Birr (James Fraher)

. . . that the first All-Ireland Hurling Final took place in Birr?

In 1865 Jonathan and Lewis Goodbody established the Clashawaun Works in Clara, thereby challenging Dundee's position as the centre of jute production in the United Kingdom and Ireland. Using imported jute from India, the factory spun fibre and then wove it into sacks. The idea to promote local employment and better living conditions was inspired by what had been achieved by other Quaker families, the Malcomsons at Portlaw and the Richardsons in Bessbrook.

The factory expanded in 1873 and, around the same time, a siding was taken off the Portarlington-Athlone Railway to make it easier to bring in raw materials and export finished products.

At its peak, more than 1,000 workers were employed at Clashawaun Works. Many had to be transported from the surrounding villages and townlands. The Goodbodys eventually built housing for their workers, resulting in the only purpose-built mill village in Offaly. In fact, the jute factory was so successful that Clara was one of the few towns in Offaly to experience population growth in the latter half of the 19th century.

The Clashawaun Works operated under the Goodbody name until 1984. Today its buildings are used as warehouses.

Left: An advertisement for products from the Clashawaun Works, 1892 (Offaly History)
Right: The Clashawaun Factory (Offaly History)

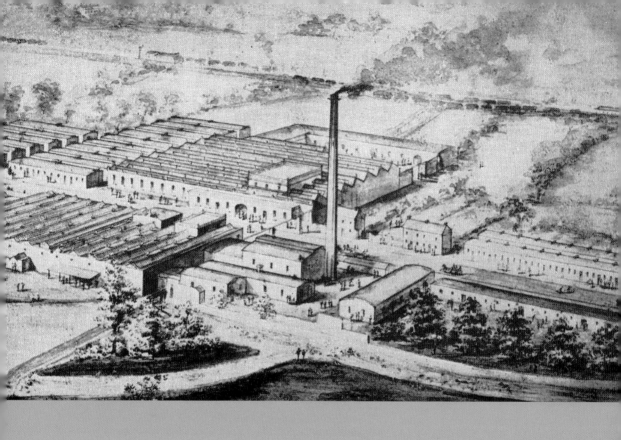

. . . that Clara once boasted Ireland's only jute factory?

The second part of the name Tullamore D.E.W. comes from the initials of Daniel Edmund Williams, who developed the whiskey into an international brand at the dawn of the 20th century.

Arriving in Tullamore as a penniless boy in the 1860s, Williams went to work at the Tullamore Distillery. Over the next two decades he developed into a valuable employee. The distillery's owner and director, Captain Bernard Daly, preferred sports to the daily grind of running a business and, by the 1880s, he was happy to leave the distillery in the more than capable hands of Williams.

As general manager, Williams was an innovator. As well as bringing electricity to Tullamore in 1893, he had the distillery install the town's first telephones. He also introduced motorised transport.

Developing the distillery's signature brand of whiskey, Williams added on his own initials: D.E.W. This inspired the slogan, 'Give every man his DEW', which is still in use today.

Left: Advertisement for Tullamore D.E.W. (Offaly History)
Right: Daniel Edmund Williams; a bottle of Tullamore D.E.W. (courtesy William Grant & Sons Irish Brands Ltd)

. . . that every bottle of Tullamore D.E.W.
bears the initials of a great businessman?

LETTERBOXES

Early wall letterboxes displayed the crown and the initials of the monarch reigning at the time they were installed, such as 'V R' for Victoria Regina (Queen Victoria, 1837-1901), 'E R' for Edward Rex (King Edward VII, 1901-10) or 'G R' for George Rex (King George V, 1910-36).

The bottom of a letterbox usually bore the name of its manufacturer. In 1881, W. T. Allen & Co. of London won the contract for the manufacture of wall letterboxes. Boxes manufactured by this company always display the royal cipher and the crown on the top, with the words 'Post Office' on the hood over the opening.

After the foundation of the Irish Free State, the doors of some letterboxes were replaced with new ones that displayed the harp and the letters 'S E' for Saorstát Eireann (Irish Free State). One of the first acts of the new Irish government was to order that the colour of letterboxes change from red to green. Also, instead of a king or queen's initials, letterboxes in the newly independent Ireland were often emblazoned with 'P & T' for Posts and Telegraphs.

Left: Tullamore letterbox with V R, the royal cipher for Queen Victoria (Amanda Pedlow)
Right: The wall letterbox at Durrow displays the royal cipher of George V along with the symbols of the Irish Free State on its door (Caimin O'Brien)
Middle Right: Aghancon lamp letterbox with the words LETTERS ONLY above the letter opening (Caimin O'Brien)
Far Right: The door of the wall letterbox at Clara displays the intertwined cipher of Edward VII (Caimin O'Brien)

. . . that letterboxes are more political than you thought?

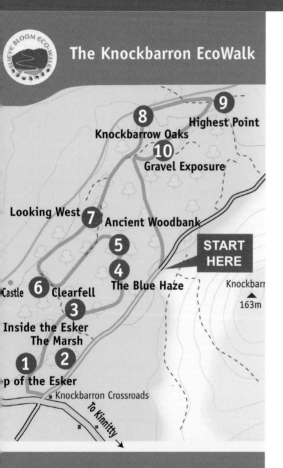

The Knockbarron EcoWalk

SLIEVE BLOOM ECO WALK

8 Knockbarrow Oaks

9 Highest Point

10 Gravel Exposure

Looking West **7** Ancient Woodbank

5

4 The Blue Haze

START HERE

Knockbarr

▲ 163m

Castle **6** Clearfell

3

Inside the Esker
The Marsh

1 **2**

p of the Esker

■ Knockbarron Crossroads

To Kinnitty

Eskers are long snake-like ridges many metres high which are distinctive in the Offaly landscape. They are made up of bouldery sediment laid down in the beds of torrential rivers that flowed at the base of the melting glaciers at the end of the Ice Age, 12,000 or so years ago. When the ice melted away, the beds of these rivers were stranded above the surrounding landscape. However, the esker ridges are often draped with extensive swathes of sand and gravel that were washed into the meltwater lakes that were such a prominent feature of the early post-glacial landscape of Offaly.

An excellent place to see a beautifully-preserved esker complex (without the later blanket of sand and gravel) is at Knockbarron near Kinnitty, which has some of the most intact eskers anywhere in the country. There is a signed Eco-Walk.

Right: Bluebells in Knockbarron (Rachel McKenna)

. . . that Offaly has some of the finest eskers in Europe?

On Tuesday the 10th May, 1785, just two years after the first hot air balloons were launched in France, 'an English adventurer' released a hot air balloon in Tullamore.

The contraption crashed into a row of houses on Patrick Street (then Barrack Street). Raging with 'ungovernable fury', fire engulfed and burned to the ground as many as 130 houses and businesses.

Walker's Hibernian Magazine expressed disgust that property had been lost and people left homeless or ruined because of such a frivolous incident. Two years later, the Methodist leader John Wesley wrote in his journal: 'I once more visited my old friends at Tullamore. Have all the balloons in Europe done so much good as can counterbalance the harm which one of them did here a year or two ago?'

The great balloon fire coincided with the ascendancy of the new landlord, Charles William Bury, later Lord Charleville. In the devastated areas, he began his life's work of remodelling and expanding Tullamore. By the time of his death in 1835, the centre of Tullamore looked much as it does today, with many fine buildings, including the courthouse, gaol and Charleville Square.

Left: The key role of this event in Tullamore's history is reflected in the crest for Tullamore Town Council with the Phoenix rising from the fire
Right: Ballooning over Tullamore in more recent years (Andy Mason)

. . . that about one-third of Tullamore's houses were destroyed following the crash of a hot-air balloon?

This is the memorial of a hurler from Killoughy called Michael Duigan, who died at the age of 27 in 1801, 83 years before the foundation of the GAA.

His tombstone is decorated with a hurl or hurling stick and a sliotar or hurling ball. The hurl is located above the S of the I H S, (which stands for the Greek name for Jesus Christ). The sliotar can be seen in the angle of the cross rising from the H.

According to local folklore, Michael Duigan was killed accidentally on a Sunday while practicing for a hurling match.

Michael Duigan Memorial (Caimin O'Brien)

. . . that Michael Duigan, Killoughy hurler, died in 1801?

The red squirrel is native to Ireland. The grey squirrel only arrived in 1911 when six pairs from Canada were presented as a wedding present in Lord Granard's family home in Longford. It is not known if these were the only grey squirrels brought in but the population has been expanding and outcompeting the red squirrels for the past 100 years . . . until now.

Recent research in Offaly has shown that where there is a strong presence of pine martens the grey squirrels have dramatically declined and the red squirrel is making a comeback.

Left: Red Squirrel (Paul Whiteley)
Right: Pine Marten (Maurice Flynn)

*. . . that red squirrels seem to thrive
alongside pine martens?*

Between 1830 and 1838, many Catholic farmers refused to pay church taxes, known as tithes, for the upkeep of the the Protestant Church of Ireland, which was the established state church at this time. This campaign of nonpayment of church tithes was known as the Tithe War. In 1835, Thomas Tiquin, a miller from Kilcomin, near Shinrone, was arrested when he refused to pay tithes due to Reverend William Brownlow Savage, Rector of Shinrone, Kilcomin and Kilmurry.

Mr Tiquin was imprisoned in the Four Courts Marshalsea gaol where he died in 1837. The political supporters of his cause organised a public funeral procession from Dublin to All Saints' graveyard, which was the traditional burial ground of the Tiquin family. The procession stopped overnight at Kildare, then went on to Mountrath, Co. Laois, and spent the final night at Birr, before the burial the following day. On Sunday, the 2nd June 1837, Thomas Tiquin was buried in All Saints' Graveyard.

The Leinster Express newspaper recorded that around 200,000 people attended this funeral, while other commentators suggested that only 200 people came out in Mountrath to see the funeral procession. In 1838, the Irish Parliament passed an Act resolving the issues of the Tithe War and Thomas Tiquin became known as 'The Last Tithe Martyr'.

Thomas Tiquin memorial (Caimin O'Brien)

BROTHER THOMAS
WHOSE REMAINS WAS CONSIGNED
TO THIS MOUND BY OVER 10000 PEOPLE
WHO VALUED HIS WORTH
HE DIED IN GAOL IN THE YEAR 37
OR TAKING PART AGAINST THE TITH
R.I.P.

. . . that this is the memorial of 'The Last Tithe Martyr'?

When John A. Killaly joined the Grand Canal Company as an assistant engineer in 1794, no one had ever constructed a canal through extensive bogland. Killaly met this challenge by supervising the most difficult part of the canal's construction. Near Edenderry, he oversaw the segment of the canal that crosses deep bogs west of the 20th lock at Ticknevin.

By 1798, Killaly had risen to chief engineer of the Grand Canal Company. He went on to complete the canal line from Tullamore to Shannon Harbour on the River Shannon. On the 25th October 1803, the navigation was officially declared to be open.

In 1810, Killaly left the Grand Canal Company. As engineer to the Directors-General of Inland Navigation, he designed and oversaw implementation of navigation routes throughout Ireland, including the Royal Canal, the Upper Shannon Navigation, the Lough Allen Canal, the Erne Navigation and the Corrib, Lagan, Newry and Suir Navigations. As well as surveying the route of the Ulster Canal, Killaly was an advisor on the extension of the Grand Canal to Ballinasloe.

Killaly died in Tullamore in 1832. A memorial erected by his wife is in St Patrick's Cathedral.

Left: The memorial in St Patrick's Cathedral, Dublin (Amanda Pedlow)
Right: An excerpt from *The Grand Canal Lines through the County of Offaly drawn by John Killaly in the year 1807;* there is one bound copy of these maps in Offaly County Library courtesy of Waterways Ireland

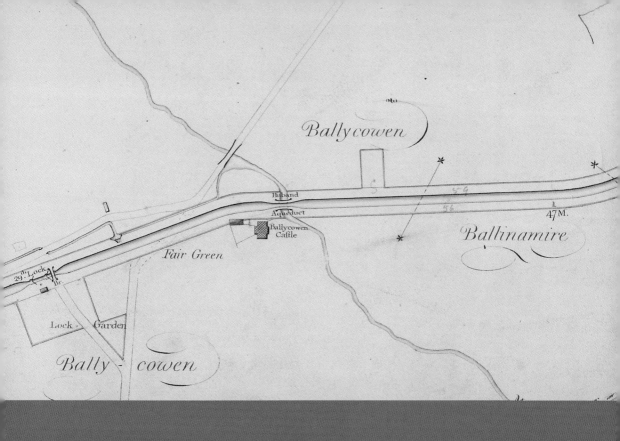

Ballycowen

Ballinamire

1/47 M.

Husband

Aqueduct

Ballycowen
Castle

Fair Green

29th Lock

Br.

Lock - Garden

Bally - cowen

*. . . that one of Ireland's brilliant engineers brought
the Grand Canal to Tullamore?*

175

As war gripped Europe in the early 1940s, Ireland suffered fuel shortages. In response, the government turned to the turf resources of the midlands.

At Turraun, the Turf Development Board built a factory that produced a petrol substitute. The fuel was created by extracting a gas from carbon made from burning peat. The plant was built in August 1941 and operated for almost two years. Many lorries came to rely upon this fuel. Today all that remains of the factory are two ivy covered walls.

Turraun was also home to one of 14 residential camps in the midlands that accommodated the workers who harvested more than three million tons of peat during this time. The peat from Turraun was shipped, via the Grand Canal, to Dublin, where it was sold from huge ricks in the Phoenix Park.

In 1946 Bord na Móna took over from the Turf Development Board. Changing its production from sod peat to milled peat, Turraun supplied the Ferbane Power Station until it ceased operation. Today the cutaway peatlands at the Turraun site is part of the Lough Boora Parklands.

Left: An excursion to the Turraun Charcoal plant (courtesy Eamon Dooley)
Right: The support walls of the plant in the late 20th century (courtesy Eamon Dooley)

. . . that these two walls are the remains of a factory that made much needed fuel during World War II?

Croghan Hill is the root of an ancient volcano that rose out of the deep ocean floor around 340 million years ago. Most of the rock of which the hill is made is either basalt (which is the now-frozen lava that once flowed out of the volcano) or volcanic ash and rocky debris thrown out of the volcanic neck while it was erupting. If you examine the stone of which the field walls around Croghan are made, you can easily find specimens of each of these rock types.

There was also extensive volcanic activity in the Limerick area, and there were other volcanoes elsewhere in the midlands that have been worn away almost to nothing. At the time there was a volcanic island arc in this part of the world similar to the Japanese Archipelago today.

Left: Croghan Hill (James Fraher)
Right: Croghan erupting by Jock Nichol (oil on canvas, 2011) from
Croghan, by John Feehan (2011)

. . . that Croghan Hill is a volcano?

The Noggus Erratic is a granite erratic boulder which was carried all the way from Connemara to Offaly in the grip of a glacier more than a kilometre thick. This erratic only came to light a few years ago because it lay out of sight on top of the moraine (rocky debris left behind after the ice melted) until Bord na Móna had stripped away the several metres of peat that accumulated on top of it after the Ice Age.

Just off the road between Clara and Tullamore there is an enormous erratic block of limestone known as the Erry Mass Rock perched on the very crest of the esker. Mass Rocks were used during the Penal Times (1700-1829) when Catholics were forbidden to celebrate or attend Mass. This is no ordinary Mass Rock, it stands 3 m above ground level and measures 5 m across. It is the biggest glacial erratic in Offaly. Its great size gives us some idea of the enormous power of the torrent that trundled it along the bed of a meltwater tunnel at the base of the glacier some 12,000 years ago.

The sketch of the erratic was done by George du Noyer around 1865. The erratic stands beside the road between Clonmacnoise and Ballinahown. Notice how the weight of the erratic has prevented erosion of the underlying till, providing a rough measure of the rate of soil erosion since the end of the Ice Age.

Top Left: George du Noyer's sketch from *A Description of the Soil – Geology of Ireland* (Dublin, 1907)
Bottom Left: The Noggus Erratic (John Feehan)
Right: Erry Mass Rock (James Fraher)

. . . that great blocks of stone stranded by melting glaciers feature in Offaly's landscape?

One of the last public executions in Ireland was of Laurence King, who was hanged in 1865 outside Tullamore Gaol. Public executions became illegal in 1868. However, hanging was still allowed within the walls of the gaol. Two years later, Lawrence and Margaret Shiel were hanged within the walls of the gaol, becoming the first people to be executed under the new law.

The second last woman to be hanged in Ireland was Mary Daly, aged 40, who was convicted of the murder of her husband and then executed in Tullamore Gaol on the 9th January 1903. Her co-accused was hanged two days later in Kilkenny.

Ireland's last execution took place in 1954. Afterwards, every death sentence was commuted by the President of Ireland until capital punishment was abolished in 1990.

Left: Governor's residence (Offaly History)
Right: Tullamore Gaol (Offaly History)

. . . that one of Ireland's last public hangings took place at Tullamore Gaol?

Brick Making

The brick industry in Offaly was concentrated in the Brosna Callows where there was suitable clay up to 5 m deep in places. The bricks have a distinctive yellow colour acquired from the firing process.

The extension of the Grand Canal west of Tullamore opened up a transport route and production increased during the 1800s. Small family-operated businesses stretched along the line of the Grand Canal from Ballycowan to Rahan, Pollagh and on towards Falsk and Gallen. At one time there were 13 brickyards in Pollagh and around a dozen in Gallen. Many of the housing schemes in Dublin suburbs between the two World Wars, such as at Dolphin's Barn and Portobello, used Gallen bricks.

With increased mechanisation elsewhere and the introduction of the concrete block, the brick making industry in Offaly declined.

Left: Gallen bricks (Rachel McKenna)
Right: Brick Making at Gallen in the early 20th century, courtesy of Maura Corcoran in *The Geology of the Laois and Offaly* by John Feehan (2013)

. . . that brick making was an important industry in west Offaly?

In the 1840s, William Parsons, the 3rd Earl of Rosse, created The Leviathan, the largest and most powerful telescope on Earth. Its lens revealed the spiral nature of some galaxies and showed objects more than ten million light years away. Looking through the 72-inch reflecting telescope in the 1840s, the Earl discovered the Whirlpool Nebula.

Eager to view and use The Leviathan, hundreds of astronomers journeyed to Birr from around the world. The telescope remained the largest in the world until 1917. Today, it is a major attraction for visitors to Birr Castle Demesne.

In recognition of the Earl's astronomical genius, his statue was made by sculptor John Henry Foley. It was unveiled by the Earl's widow, Mary Rosse—herself a pioneer of early photography—in 1876.

The Earl's achievement was summed up by Patrick Moore in *Eyes on the Universe* (1997): 'Alone and unaided, the third Earl made what was by far the most powerful telescope ever constructed, and used it to such good effect that he was able to see further, and more clearly, than anyone before him. Nothing of the sort had ever happened before; nothing of the sort can ever happen again'.

Left: The Statue of William Parsons by John Henry Foley (James Fraher)
The Latin inscription on the plinth translates as:
This Birr man illuminated the ramparts of the universe with his telescope.
Now his name is carried to the stars of God.
Right: The Leviathan (courtesy Birr Scientific and Heritage Foundation)

. . . that for over 75 years, the greatest telescope in the world could be found at Birr?

From 1848 until 1886, a building on O'Connor Square, where the Bridge Centre is today, was a tobacco factory. Owned by Quaker brothers T.P. and R. Goodbody, it spun about 4,000 pounds of imported leaf each day into tobacco for pipes, cigarettes and snuff.

The Goodbody factory sold tobacco under the brand names Bird's Eye, Golden Flake, York River and Quaker Twist. Its snuffs were called Cork, Brown and High Toast.

By 1883, the factory was processing one million pounds of tobacco each year. It employed 220 workers, including six travellers on the road, and operated branch offices in Dublin, Limerick and Liverpool. After the malting and distilling businesses, the tobacco factory was Tullamore's largest employer.

When an accidental fire burned the factory in 1886, the Goodbodys decided to move the entire business— including all their employees—to a ready-made building in the Harold's Cross area of Dublin. This was a blow to Tullamore; over the next five years its population dropped by nearly 14 percent. There was a silver lining: shortly after the Goodbody tobacco factory fire, the people of Tullamore set up a voluntary fire brigade to deal with similar disasters in the future.

Left: Goodbody's Golden Flake Tin (Michael Goodbody)
Right: Goodbody's tobacco factory (courtesy of the National Library of Ireland; M6/26)

. . . that Tullamore had a tobacco factory?

This fine building, used today as a guesthouse of Mount St Joseph Abbey, may incorporate portions of the 17th-century home of Richard Heaton, recognized as the first recording botanist known to have lived in Ireland.

Richard Heaton came from Yorkshire, was educated at Cambridge and was then ordained. He came to live in Ireland in the 1630s. During journeys to the Burren he recorded abundant quantities of mountain avens and blue gentian.

Heaton died at Ballyskenagh in 1666. Afterwards, his son renamed the property Mount Heaton. The estate passed into the hands of the Armstrong family, who retained it until 1816, when William Armstrong lost the entire property in a card game to the Duke of York. During the same game, the Duke went on to lose Mount Heaton to General Taylor.

In 1877 Arthur Moore purchased 600 acres of the original Heaton property for the Cistercians of Mount St Joseph.

Mount Saint Joseph Abbey walled garden and guesthouse, near Shinrone (James Fraher)

*. . . that Ireland's first recording botanist lived
in what is now Mount St Joseph Abbey?*

WORLD'S FIRST AUTOMOBILE FATALITY

The first person to die as the result of an automobile accident was scientist and author Mary Ward, who perished in Birr in 1869. Mary Ward was one of four passengers in a steam-powered automobile, designed and built by William Parsons, the 3rd Earl of Rosse. When the driver, Richard Biggs, turned a corner, Mary Ward fell from the car and was severely injured. She was taken to the home of a local physician, but died almost immediately.

After the accident, the automobile was broken up and destroyed. No pictures of it survive. An inquest found that Mary Ward's death was the result of an accident.

A cousin of the Earl of Rosse, Mary Ward was a well-known scientist, artist, naturalist and author. She published three scientific books, and numerous articles, and was one of three women of her day to receive the monthly notices of the Royal Astronomers' Society. She was also the mother of eight children. Mary Ward is the only non-lineal Parsons relative to be buried in the Parsons' family vault in Birr.

Left: Portrait of Mary Ward (courtesy of the Birr Scientific and Heritage Foundation)
Right: Map of Birr Town by Uto Hogerzeil showing the route of the automobile until the crash (drawn by Uto Hogerzeil)

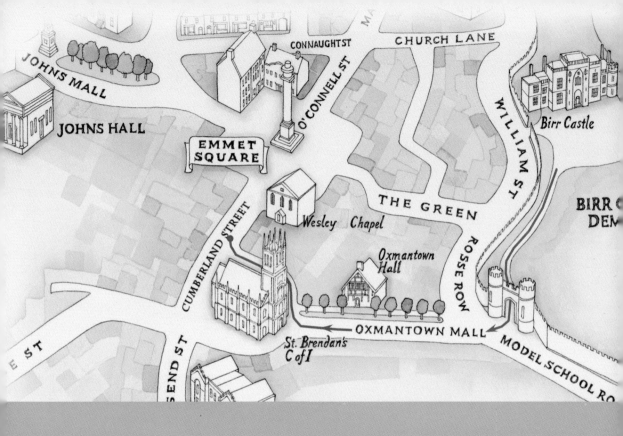

. . . that the world's first automobile fatality
occurred in Birr?

Michael Scott

In the 1930s, Irish architect Michael Scott, with his business partner Norman Good, designed and built the Tullamore General Hospital. The building, which features strong horizontal lines and makes use of local materials, reflects the international style of the time, as well as Dutch modernist architecture.

Scott is best known for his masterwork, the Busáras in Store Street, Dublin. However, he designed several buildings in and around Tullamore. Using Clonaslee stone for a façade, he designed the Williams shop in Patrick Street. He also built Shepherd's Wood at Screggan and an attractive bungalow, faced in Clonaslee stone, on the Charleville Road. Along with Good, Scott designed and built the vocational school at Clonaslee.

In the 1940s, Scott guided the refurbishment of the Jesuit Chapel at Tullabeg. Today the altar that he designed for that building, made in native oak with carvings by Laurence Campbell, can be seen in St Colman's Church at Mucklagh.

Left: The altar from Tullabeg, now in Mucklagh Church (Sarah Gavin)
Right: Tullamore Hospital in the 1940s (Offaly History)

*. . . that the Tullamore General Hospital was designed
by one of the most important Irish architects
of the 20th century?*

The famine of 1433 was so horrendous that the year was later called 'the summer of death'. Some relief came at Killeigh, where Margaret O'Carroll hosted two great assemblies to feed the desperate people.

On the 26th March, over 2,700 people from Ireland and Scotland, including the poor and members of mendicant orders, gathered at Killeigh's abbey. At two great feasts, sponsored by Margaret, guests received 'meates, moneyes and all manner of gifts'. Wearing a gold dress, Margaret supervised the events from the attic rooms of the abbey. On the ground below, her husband, Calvagh O'Connor, who was mounted on horseback, made sure that all guests were served.

That same day, Margaret donated two golden chalices to the church and agreed to foster two orphans. Ever after, she was known as 'the hospitable O'Carroll'.

Left: An artist's interpretation of the great feast given at Killeigh by Margaret O'Carroll, wife of Calvagh O'Connor, Lord of Offaly, on St Sincheall's Day 1433, from L. M. McCrait's book *The Romance of Irish Heroines* (1913)
Right: Killeigh Church (James Fraher)

*. . . that in 1433 a great woman of Offaly
fed the starving people of Ireland?*

In 697 Adomnán, the abbot of Iona, assembled 91 powerful clerics and chieftains at Birr. Together they passed the Law of the Innocents, also known as Cáin Adomnáin, which exempted women and children, as well as priests, from military service in times of war.

Cáin Adomnáin established the protection of women as a matter of law. It specified penalties for crimes against women, such as sexual harassment, rape, physical harm or murder. The law read: '…no woman is deprived of her testimony, if it be bound in righteous deeds. For a mother is a venerable treasure… an increase in the Kingdom of Heaven, a propagation on earth'.

In 1997, Birr celebrated the 1300th anniversary of Cáin Adomnáin. Among the artefacts commemorating this occasion were a wooden cross carved by Rev Bro Anthony, OSB, a manuscript copy of the Cáin by scribe Margaret Maher, and a replica medieval bell by blacksmith Dan Edwards.

Left: Wooden cross (James Fraher)
Right: Bell and manuscript (Amanda Pedlow)

. . . that one of the first laws protecting women
and children was passed in Birr?

Just outside Clara is one of the rarest and most important ecosystems in Western Europe: a raised bog.

Scoured by glaciers during the last Ice Age, this was once a shallow lake. Approximately 8,000 years ago, the lake became overgrown with reeds and in time the area turned into a fen. Then, as decaying plant growth choked the fen, mosses took over and the bog was born. The bog laid down so much peat that eventually it rose above the surrounding landscape.

Today snipe and curlew find cover in the heathery dry areas, while skylarks soar in the skies above. Dragonflies and damselflies live part of their life cycle in the bog's pools. One butterfly, the Large Heath, depends on the raised bog for its survival, although many other butterflies and moths can be spotted there.

Clara Bog has a number of soaks: mineral-rich pools and small lakes that support plant life. Dominated by sphagnum moss and other mosses, soaks are also home to sedges, including common cottongrass and deergrass.

A wooden boardwalk enables visitors to venture into Clara Bog and view its rare ecosystem up close. To find out more, visit the Clara Bog Visitor Centre, which is co-located with Clara Library.

Images of Clara Bog (courtesy National Parks and Wildlife Service)

. . . that Clara bog is one of Western Europe's few surviving raised bogs?

The cast iron entrance gates to the Courthouse and the old Gaol in Tullamore are decorated with bundles of sharpened sticks, bound with cord. Axes extend from some of the bundles.

They are called fasces, from the Latin word fascis, meaning bundle. For the Etruscans (circa 900 to 400 BC), fasces symbolised the power and authority of a magistrate or judge. Fasces also stood for the concept of 'strength in unity', for while a single stick is easily broken, a bundle is less easily so. When they adopted the fasces, the Romans added an axe to represent an magistrate's authority to levy the death penalty.

By the time the Courthouse and Gaol received its first prisoners in 1830, fasces had long been used to ornament buildings used in the criminal justice system. Less than a century later, Mussolini embraced the symbol of fasces, and the name of these bundles gave rise to the political term *fascism*.

Roman Lictor.

Left: Vintage engraving of an ancient Roman lictor, who carried a fasces on his left shoulder (courtesy Duncan Walker)
Right: The entrance gates to Kilcruttin Business Park, formerly Tullamore Gaol (James Fraher)

*. . . that this ancient symbol for justice ornaments
the gates of the old Tullamore Gaol?*

In the 1980s, as he travelled the bog road from Clonbulloge towards Daingean, Henry Edgill stopped his car for a moment and stepped out. Suddenly, a blazing light lit up his surroundings. Hearing a fast, whistling sound, Edgill turned just in time to see a meteorite hurtling about 25 m away toward Earth. Bushes prevented him from seeing its impact as it hit the bog.

Edgill returned home feeling slightly shaken, but unhurt. This, unfortunately, was not the case with the two other known meteor strikes in Offaly, which were recorded during the 19th century.

At Cloneen near Dowris in 1828, a 'meteoric stone containing iron, nickel and copper' fell from the sky, killing two young brothers—John and Patrick Horan— who were in a field making a stack of oats.

Then, in the 1830s or 40s, a meteorite crashed through the roof of the local mill at the Rapemills, between Birr and Banagher. It blew out the windows, 'threw down the lofts' and killed the miller, Mr Woods.

. . . that at least three meteorites have struck Offaly?

GPS Locations

A number of the sites featured are on private lands. Many of sites that can be seen or visited are listed below. Please check with www.offaly.ie/heritage for further visitor information or email heritage@offalycoco.ie with specific queries.

Subject	Sat Nav Co-ordinates
All-Ireland Final Statue, Birr	53 05 21.0 N 07 54 30.5 W
Ardara Bridge, Cadamstown	53 07 36.4 N 07 39 37.2 W
Belmont Bridge	53 15 01.2 N 07 53 27.9 W
Birr Castle Demesne	53 05 43.9 N 07 54 50.7 W
Birr Library	53 05 38.2 N 07 54 29.7 W
Blundell Aqueduct	53 19 42.0 N 07 02 10.4 W
Blundell Hill, Edenderry	53 20 23.4 N 07 03 07.0 W
Boher Church and Shrine	53 19 28.9 N 07 43 41.6 W
Boland's Lock House, Tullamore	53 16 47.6 N 07 27 58.2 W
Charleville Castle, Tullamore	53 15 37.7 N 07 31 40.4 W
Charleville Demesne, King Oak	53 15 54.2 N 07 30 35.3 W
Church of the Assumption, Tullamore	53 16 36.1 N 07 29 24.2 W
Clara Bog and Library	53 20 31.5 N 07 37 03.0 W
Clareen Rag Tree	53 04 01.7 N 07 47 40.1 W
Clonmacnoise	53 19 28.6 N 07 59 17.7 W
Coffin Rests, Roscomroe	53 01 45.0 N 07 45 16.8 W
Column in Emmet Square, Birr	53 05 46.0 N 07 54 39.0 W
Crinkill Barracks	53 04 42.8 N 07 53 42.6 W
Daingean Courthouse	53 17 40.3 N 07 17 32.5 W
Dan and Molly's, Ballyboy	53 10 25.4 N 07 41 48.8 W
Edenderry Library, Sheela-na-Gig	53 20 34.4 N 07 02 52.6 W
Fahy near Rhode, Windmill (view from road)	53 21 07.1 N 07 10 30.5 W
Gallen Graveyard	53 15 47.7 N 07 49 21.2 W
Gallen Slabs	53 15 53.1 N 07 49 26.9 W
Geashill Village	53 14 08.6 N 07 19 20.8 W
Glebe Walk, Geashill	53 14 14.1 N 07 19 36.6 W

Glenregan Lime Kiln	53 05 23.0 N 07 38 58.2 W
John's Mall, Birr, 3rd Earl of Rosse Statue	53 05 44.4 N 07 54 29.6 W
Kilcormac Pietà	53 10 38.3 N 07 43 35.7 W
Killaderry, Daingean	53 18 30.0 N 07 17 08.1 W
Killeigh	53 12 49.4 N 07 27 03.2 W
Kinnitty High Cross	53 06 10.4 N 07 41 50.9 W
Kinnitty Pyramid	53 05 46.1 N 07 43 12.0 W
Knockbarron Esker Walk	53 06 39.7 N 07 45 36.3 W
Lemanaghan Monastic Site	53 17 34.6 N 07 44 37.4 W
Lough Boora Parklands	53 12 58.4 N 07 43 32.6 W
Lusmagh, Windmill (view from road)	53 10 05.4 N 08 01 21.1 W
Manchester Martyrs' Monument, Birr	53 05 36.3 N 07 54 46.0 W
Maurice Harron's Saints and Scholars Sculptures	53 18 14.9 N 07 29 26.8 W
Molloy's Thatch House, Killurin (view from road)	53 12 30.2 N 07 30 50.2 W
Monegall	52 52 46.9 N 07 57 28.7 W
Mount St Joseph Monastery	52 57 51.8 N 07 51 23.7 W
Mucklagh Church	53 15 14.8 N 07 32 23.2 W
Oxmantown Mall, Birr	53 05 52.9 N 07 54 35.4 W
Pilgrims' Path cycle route, Ballycumber	53 19 35.2 N 07 41 10.5 W
Pollagh church	53 16 38.0 N 07 42 46.7 W
Sculpture in the Parklands	53 12 58.4 N 07 43 32.6 W
Silver River, Cadamstown	53 07 36.4 N 07 39 37.2 W
Srah Castle, Tullamore (view from tow path)	53 16 32.7 N 07 30 32.8 W
St Carthage's Church, Rahan	53 16 44.6 N 07 36 45.1 W
St Paul's Church of Ireland & Charlotte's Way B&B, Banagher,	53 11 02.4 N 07 58 47.3 W
St Rynagh's Church, Banagher	53 11 10.4 N 07 58 52.7 W
Tullamore D.E.W. Visitor Centre	53 16 39.5 N 07 29 35.4 W
Tullamore Hospital	53 16 58.4 N 07 29 26.3 W
Tullamore Gaol now Kilcruttin Business Park	53 16 13.9 N 07 29 49.2 W
Tullamore Star Fort	53 16 33.4 N 07 29 41.8 W